HELP & HOPE FOR PREGNANT TEENS

Practical Advice for Teenagers, Parents, Teachers, Pastors, Counselors, and Friends

KAREN J. SANDVIG

Regal Books
A Division of GL Publications
Ventura, California, U.S.A.

For all of you who have cared for, supported, guided, prayed for, believed in, and loved me—especially Him! I love you, too.

Published by Regal Books
A Division of GL Publications
Ventura, California 93006
Printed in U.S.A.

Scripture quotations in this book are taken from the *HOLY BIBLE: NEW INTERNATIONAL VERSION*. Copyright © 1973, 1978, 1984 by the International Bible Society. Used by permission of Zondervan Bible Publishers.

© Copyright 1988 by Karen J. Sandvig
All rights reserved.

Library of Congress Cataloging-in-Publication Data

Sandvig, Karen J., 1956-
You're what?!

1. Teenage mothers—United States—Life skills guides. 2. Motherhood—Religious aspects—Christianity. 3. Teenage marriage—United States. 4. Teenage pregnancy. I. Title.
HQ759.4.S26 1988 306.7'088055 88-3056
ISBN 0-8307-1267-4

2 3 4 5 6 7 8 9 10/ 91 90 89 88

Rights for publishing this book in other languages are contracted by Gospel Literature International (GLINT) foundation. GLINT also provides technical help for the adaptation, translation, and publishing of Bible study resources and books in scores of languages worldwide. For further information, contact GLINT, Post Office Box 488, Rosemead, California, 91770, U.S.A., or the publisher.

Contents

Introduction

Jenny had her sixteenth birthday party last month. She's a pretty girl, with blond hair that swings to her waist. Her big blue eyes twinkle when she smiles. She is an honor roll student, plays the flute in the school band and is an active member of the youth group at church.

Jenny has been dating Brad for several months. Both teenagers are from middle-class families. There are no remarkable problems in their lives. Actually, their futures look quite bright. However, this afternoon there was a frightening shadow cast on Jenny, and on Brad, for that matter. Jenny found out she is pregnant.

While lying across her bed this evening, tears stream down Jenny's face. Panic, loneliness and confusion fill her heart. What will she do? How can she tell her parents? Will Brad still love her? Who will help her? Why—oh, *why*—has this happened to her?

Jenny is not alone. One in four teenage girls gets

pregnant—more than a million young ladies—in the United States annually. In 1980, this figure was one in ten. Even with billions of dollars spent on sex education, the teen pregnancy rate continues to rise.

America has an epidemic of children conceiving children. Once a teen is pregnant, the results are irrevocable. No matter what course of action she takes, there will be effects on several lives for many years.

These kids and their families need help—gentle, professional guidance to work through the urgent problems that face them—so that they can begin to gradually piece their lives together again.

Jenny's parents, when she tells them of her pregnancy, are devastated. Her father, overcome with initial rage, slams his chair back from the table and storms out of the house.

Jenny's mother's face turns ashen and she whispers, "Go to your room, Jenny. Just go to your room!"

As Jenny drags herself upstairs, she hears her mother's sobs; she feels like the worst sort of traitor.

The answers to the problems surrounding teenage sexual activity and pregnancy lie with the Ultimate Healer—God, through His Son, Jesus Christ, and His Word to mankind, the Bible. God has also sent us a great Counselor, the Holy Spirit, to guide us through the difficult changes, experiences, and consequences of poor choices during adolescence.

There are no issues too frightening or hopeless for God. He has given us His will for our direction in all things, including teenage sexual conduct, abstinence, pregnancy, abortion, and every complex circumstance we might be faced with.

Prayer is our 24-hour talk line to God. Combined with the powerful communication of the Holy Spirit, prayer brings us into God's presence through Christ. In this spiritual communion we can determine God's step-by-step intentions for us as we lead the teenagers in our lives.

Christian ways of coping with pregnant teens like Jenny, selecting options that are available to them, getting help, overcoming common pitfalls, handling teenage marriage, birthing a child, and why young girls get pregnant in the first place will be explored in *You're What?! Help and Hope for Pregnant Teens.*

CHAPTER ONE

Why Teenage Girls Get Pregnant

Do you remember when you first noticed that the girls in school had changed from *nerds* to *babes?* And, the boys went from *gross* to *hot?*

As anyone knows, with puberty comes the onslaught of surging hormones, the awakening of feelings never before experienced—both physical and emotional. Just brushing arms with a special someone can create electrical currents in a teen's body. Dances in the school gym on Friday nights trigger a heaviness in the loins that surprise and confuse even stable youth. Certain songs, smells or settings start sensations in the mind and body. Whether it's a rock 'n' roll tune or a football game, teen years are the most carefree—and the most vulnerable.

PERSONALITY CHANGES AND POOR CHOICES

For Lynn, an especially rebellious, insecure teen, the

intensity of her emotions confuses her so much she doesn't know how to cope. The pain of adjusting to home, school, peers, and her changing self is nearly unbearable. Lynn knows that one of the few things that makes her feel good is being with a boy. She may be nervous, self-conscious, and lacking in confidence—but, above all, she feels good.

The exaggerated sensations of youth can be extremely pleasurable for the moment, or they can be deadly. Shelly's mercurial nature makes her so susceptible to whatever she's feeling on a given day that she can be prompted to use drugs, drink alcohol, drive a car dangerously fast, engage in a sexual relationship, or, possibly, take her own life.

Lynn and Shelly are perfectly nice teens from perfectly nice homes. But they can fall prey to the dangers of adolescence. They do not necessarily enjoy their experiences with the forbidden, including sexual encounters. They are so overwhelmed by their hormonal stirrings that they feel estranged from the self they used to be, and have trouble controlling their actions.

The need to be loved, strongest of all human drives, often demands gratification at the crux of all this turbulence, no matter what the cost. When this drive is most potent, teens are in their ultimate time of need, a sort of *holding zone* where they want desperately to know they are loved, yet don't feel very lovable.

Unfortunately, it is at this same time that teenagers' attitudes make it hard to act lovingly toward them. They can be so moody, unpredictable, and uncooperative that it is difficult for adults to be civilized with them, much less give them unconditional love.

Lori is a veritable caldron of simmering emotions, and often finds herself in precarious positions. She doesn't understand her feelings, and is rarely able to verbalize them. The paradox is too much for her. One minute, she wants to lay her head in her mother's lap and cry, as she did when she was little, the next minute she is raging at her parents for not allowing her to go on a co-ed weekend to the mountains.

It is at this stage of life that girls come to a fork in the path of growing up. One direction leads toward healthy adulthood with a normal spattering of problems along the way. The other leads to major life difficulties, such as teen pregnancy.

Even girls who feel genuinely loved, secure, and an integral part of their families may send forth distress signals. Watchful, perceptive parents can pick up on these signals and, often, guide their teens wisely onto the healthy path.

However, those girls who do not have the advantage of sensitive parents may choose the pathway of challenge that is very rough indeed. Sometimes it's not a matter of insensitivity on the parts of parents. Rather, it is the fact that the frantic pace of modern living gets the best of many well-meaning parents. Teenagers' problems may easily disappear under the pressures of providing food, shelter, and clothing.

Then again, the personality changes in a teen can be too much for even the most conscientious parents. Melanie's inner conflicts were so complex that her parents felt completely helpless. They had an open, sensitive, and loving home. Melanie, who had been a cheerful, well-adjusted child, was so adversely affected by adolescent changes that her parents could no longer understand her. She became a stranger in their home. They did not know how to run interference for her so that she could cope with her hormonal changes. She got pregnant. Professional help guided the family through this ordeal and helped Melanie back onto the pathway that, with her parents' support, led her to become an emotionally stable young woman.

LACK OF SEX EDUCATION AT HOME

Probably the biggest safeguard against indiscriminate sexual behavior is for parents to maintain an open, conversational attitude about sex in their home, where sex is naturally regarded, just as any other topic of priority.

Ellen feels as comfortable asking questions about sex at home as she does about school, religion, and other family topics. Ellen is well on her way to mastering her adolescent urges because she feels secure at home.

Annie has been technically educated about her body. She knows the mechanics of sex, birth control, and disease, but she is not necessarily better equipped to deal with sexual issues than a girl who has few details. Having all the right information does not mean Annie is ready for the responsibility of using this knowledge. She, as all kids, needs her parents—as much at fifteen as at five—in different ways.

In homes where parents encourage relaxed conversations, calm acceptance of human sexuality, and a loving approach to teen issues, a dangerous *domino*-type of events, which can alter the entire family's life, may be headed off.

THE DOMINO EFFECT

Consider Diane. A nice girl who's just had her fifteenth birthday, Diane is a typical teenager. Her family is upper middle-class, her school is a relatively safe, suburban high school, and she has not been in any notable trouble.

On any given weekday, Diane is awakened by her mother just before both parents leave for work. Diane gets herself ready and off to school on her own.

One particular Friday when Diane arrives at school, she is horrified that her friend Jeanette has repeated a remark Diane made to her in confidence about another girl in their group. Paula, the leader of the group, has made it clear that she is hostile toward Diane. Jeanette, Teresa, and Julie follow suit. In her third class, Diane gets back a failed test paper. Her nylons tear on her seat at lunch, leaving a gaping hole at her knee. Paula and the others, who sit at the same regular table, laugh loudly at her predicament.

In physical education class, Diane discovers she's started her period and a small bloodstain is on the back of her skirt. She has no sanitary protection with her. The teacher tells her to go to the office.

In the office, there are four male classmates lining the wall opposite the reception counter. Diane tries discreetly to ask the secretary about getting a sanitary napkin, but the boys overhear what she needs. They start making rude jokes about her problem.

On top of all this, Diane begins having cramps and feels achy all over. When the dismissal bell rings, she hurries to her locker to gather her things. She slams her locker shut, shifts the pile of books she's holding, and drops one. Now she's in tears.

A popular boy, Tommy, retrieves the book for her. Seeing how badly she feels, he asks, "Are you going to be all right?"

Diane stammers something about missing her bus, and Tommy quickly says, "It's okay. I'll give you a ride home."

On the way, she tells him how embarrassed she is and how grateful for his understanding. Tommy feels pretty important—sort of like the knight who saved the day. He notices that Diane's a real cute girl. Diane thinks Tommy's got a great smile.

When they arrive at Diane's, they talk in the car for several minutes. They find they have much in common and hit it off very well. Tommy asks Diane out for a date, she accepts, and ends her day feeling so good she can hardly believe it.

Tommy and Diane are soon seeing a lot of each other, and quickly become an item. Paula and the others have long forgotten their cruelty to Diane, but she hasn't. She soothes her bruised pride by spending time between classes and at lunch with Tommy, showing the girls she doesn't need their kind of friendship.

Diane has connected with someone to love. In a teenager's abstract way, Tommy seems to be the solution to all her problems.

Diane's parents are socially active. They allow Tommy to come over when Diane is watching her younger siblings, assuming the children's presence will deter sexual impulses while they're out. However, Diane and Tommy have plenty of time, otherwise, to be alone. There are nearly three hours after school before their parents arrive home from work. And, of course, they are in Tommy's car on dates. At first, their kisses are innocent but, as the weeks go on, they lead to caresses, then petting.

As Diane falls more deeply into the relationship, changes begin to take place in her personality. Some seem deceptively well-behaved. She's up and out of bed immediately in the mornings. She gets her chores done in half the usual time. She doesn't complain about her brothers as much. Diane's parents are pleased with her brighter outlook, and joke between them that she should have had a boyfriend months ago.

Tommy starts pressuring Diane to "go all the way." She puts him off. She tells him she is afraid he won't love or respect her any more, and she isn't "that kind of girl."

Tommy convincingly points out to Diane that a sexual relationship is a natural expression of their love for each other. Diane hears a soft whispering inside her, eroding her conviction. She imagines what it would be like to make love with Tommy. Just when she gets to the limit of her experience, a sort of pinch in her stomach reminds her that she is right to stand her ground.

THE ALCOHOL/DRUG CONNECTION

One weekend Diane and Tommy attend a party at a classmate's whose parents are away. Tommy has a few beers, Diane sips one. Tommy becomes openly affectionate as the music creates a mood and someone dims the lights. He breathes in her ear that he wants her, as he holds her tight. Diane thinks she will melt into the floor. Her legs are weak, she smells Tommy's cologne, her whole body is alive with arousal, and her heart is beating wildly.

Tommy prods Diane hard to slip upstairs with him. The alcohol he has consumed has taken away his inhibitions and he is very frank about his desires. Diane recognizes the familiar warning pinch in her stomach. While someone is changing cassette tapes, Diane slips away to the bathroom.

Paula, Jeanette, and Teresa giggle at her flushed face as they all gather outside the door, waiting their turn.

Jeanette asks Diane, "What's wrong with you? Can't you wait until later to do it with Tommy?"

Diane's eyebrows raise at the realization that her

peers assume she's already made love with Tommy.

Paula remarks smartly, "If it were me dating that hunk Tommy, we would never have made it to the party—we'd be in his car somewhere!" The girls' laughter rings in Diane's ears.

She is really confused now. Have all her friends had sex? They implied they knew all about it, but nobody actually said they'd made love before. Remembering how cruel they can be, she's not about to ask, and she waits her turn in silence.

Diane feels threatened. What if she keeps holding back and Tommy breaks up with her for a more experienced girl? After all, she wants to go to bed with him. It's just that her parents have taught her that sex is an intimate, sacred relationship between two people who share their whole life—not just a physical thing. Of course, she and Tommy have shared much. Still, the pinch deep inside her remains.

Diane's stomach turns over as she walks back into the party and sees that Tommy is slow-dancing with Paula. Thoroughly agitated, she gets another glass of beer. She's got to think. A third glass of beer, and a slow warmth spreads through her body. Nobody's going to take Tommy from her!

Tommy comes to her and expresses his hope that she's not angry at him for dancing with Paula. "She came right up to me, put her arms around my neck, and started dancing," he says.

Relief floods through Diane. Tommy is innocent in the matter. She looks up at Tommy with hooded eyes and smiles. "It's okay, I'm not afraid of the competition."

When they dance again, Diane's movements are more provocative. She is aware of Tommy's body pressed against hers. The liquid fire spreading through her is too much for Diane to handle. Tommy's eyes glitter with anticipation. He loves her—she loves him—life is wonderful.

Suddenly they are in a bedroom neither has seen before. Tommy is pulling at her jeans and she's clutching at

Diane's self-control has been swallowed up by the momentum of her relationship with Tommy. There is no turning back.

his clothes. She hopes these waves of passion will never leave her. She experiences an unexpected, dull pain, then almost immediately, it's over.

For Diane, with barely 15 years of life behind her, every moral ethic she's known has been violated. In a strange bedroom, among other kids' coats, Diane's self-control has been swallowed up by the momentum of her relationship with Tommy. There is no turning back.

SUSPENDED BETWEEN TWO WORLDS

Diane is thrown into a state of limbo. On one side of her is the safety of her childhood purity. On her other side is the unknown world of adulthood that teenagers instinctively reach for. Diane is hurtled, adrift, into a chasm between the two. She cannot recoup where she stood yesterday, and she doesn't know where she will stand tomorrow.

Her quandary is complete. She sees nowhere to turn. In her young eyes she is a dirty, sinful girl, unable to forgive herself. It is nearly impossible for her to see beyond the situation. She has not lived enough life to know that all is not lost. It is hard for her to understand that time will pass—even the next several months until she can get her driver's license—much less that she can right herself after this terrifying mistake.

Diane's guilt, shame, and fear prevent her from seeking advice. To do so would require exposing her actions. There's only one person for Diane to cleave to—Tommy. One day rolls into another. Time does pass. The couple has sex again. And again.

Diane does not seek out a means of birth control. This would add further to the complex situation. *Good girls* do not plan sex—it just happens. Birth control is premeditated, which means to Diane that, if she uses it, she is not a good girl, but one of *those kinds.* Tommy doesn't think much about it at all. He's got a condom in his wallet, which his older brother gave him, jokingly, on his sixteenth birthday. He figures it's not much good now, and assumes Diane knows what she's doing.

It is important to note that, regardless of exposure to the sexual prowess teen girls see in television, moves and magazines, they still want very much to be one of the good girls. This instinctive drive to be a worthwhile, loved human being is a mockery in the web of reasons why girls get pregnant. The very things they do not do (seek advice, use birth control, etc.) cause them to be revealed as exactly what they do not want to be (sexually active). Only when a teenager gets pregnant or contracts a sexually transmitted disease does she discover the irony of her ways.

Diane and Tommy, like their counterparts in every city, town, and village across the United States, exist in a cocoon of fantasy. Family planning experts report one of the first things pregnant girls say to them is, "I never thought it would happen to me."

Teens believe themselves to be the exception to every

rule. Their love is unique, their capacity for drugs and alcohol is exempt from danger, their judgment while driving fast is invincible, their problems are bigger than anyone else's, and their participation in a sexual relationship is protected from pregnancy—they think.

ESCAPE TO FREEDOM

Diane and Tommy's relationship takes on a perpetual motion that sends them deeper into their pattern. Diane starts slacking off at school; one day she quits track; she's moodier than usual, and seems preoccupied.

Diane's parents, although there are alarm bells sounding, cannot bring themselves to confront their daughter's sexuality, and contribute the changes in her to an adolescent phase.

In the only effort they can comfortably deal with to get Diane back on track, they begin to monitor her actions more. It dawns on them that Tommy is almost her exclusive caller. They encourage her to see more of her girlfriends. They ask her lots of questions, turn her requests down more frequently, and add extra duties to her household responsibilities.

Diane resents her parents' interference. She becomes sulky, rebellious, and, sometimes, downright surly. Her parents become more critical and domineering, as their worry over Diane mounts. The tension in the home worsens to the point of crucial as, one after another, doors of communication slam shut.

Diane takes her parents' reactions as certain judgment upon her. She's sure they know what she's been doing and hate her for it. In reality they only want to deny their suspicions. Diane is full of self-hatred, false justifications, and immense anxiety.

When she gets her period each month, she is giddy with relief. She vows not to have sex with Tommy any more. But, since he is the only figure in her life who knows what's going on and still loves her, her promise is soon broken.

At some point, pregnancy starts to appeal to Diane just below her conscious level. In an irrational way, it becomes an escape—an escape from the erratic feelings at home, from the limbo in which she has existed, the battering confusion, the loneliness of having alienated her girlfriends, and from her inner misery. Just as Tommy himself was a way to solve what now seems to be very minor pressures, pregnancy becomes a way to solve her much larger problems of the present.

Desperate to keep some of her self-respect, Diane believes her relationship with Tommy is okay because they love each other. They are true to each other. If she doesn't get pregnant, then she's been lucky. If she does, well, then, come what may. A baby would be proof of their real love together.

Diane reasons that a baby can't be that much trouble, certainly no more restrictive than how she's living right now. Besides, a baby is someone to love, someone to love her back for always. She and Tommy—a family, a family for her to mold and form just the way she wants it to be. Diane's wandering thoughts become her idealistic attempt to force things to be all right.

If there are unresolved conflicts imbedded in a teen's background, it is now that they add great tumult to the details surrounding their sexual relationships and/or an ensuing pregnancy. And, in the case of the girl who has several sexual partners, there is almost always a significant combination of these conflicts in her past—for example, broken homes, where a teenage girl has not had a healthy male role model, or a home where there has been physical and/or sexual abuse. The teenager may be so compelled to attach herself to a loving family unit that she earnestly hopes for a pregnancy. Disappointed to see her period arrive each month, she may deliberately increase the level of her sexual activity in order to better her odds of conception.

She has so little self-esteem that she reaches pitifully for a way to live out her innate need to love and be loved.

In families where there are chemical dependency complications, a teen has often dealt with so much inconsistency at home that all she can think of is getting out. She is a girl who holds on tightly to a fantasy in which her life turns out to have a happily-ever-after ending. She may purposely seek a pregnancy as a means of taking control of her life. A baby of her own seems an avenue to provide the continuity and love out of which she feels she's been cheated.

SELF-ESTEEM/BEING VALUED AS SHE IS

Jan has been berated by criticism and ridicule since she was very young. She has so little self-esteem that she reaches pitifully for a way to live out her innate need to love and be loved. She has one sure channel available to her—having a baby. Her feminine ability to conceive, carry, and birth a child into the world is something all her own. Unrealistically, Jan believes that to do so will make a statement of worth about herself, especially to those whose approval and love she desires so frantically—her parents.

Cassie has been domineered to such an extent by her father that she feels like a possession, and has a great need to claim her own separate identity. To Cassie, a baby is a way to express parts of her own personality that she isn't free to express otherwise. A baby becomes a balm to Cassie's starving ego.

Lisa is from a poverty-stricken area of a major city. All her life she has known struggle and hardship. In her case, a baby is symbolic of a combination of all these things—love, escape, control of her own life, feeling worthwhile, and having her own identity. But most of all, to Lisa the idea of a baby is hope for a better tomorrow in her stressful life.

Sadly, a teenager's ability to reason can be so underdeveloped that she is somewhat like the first-time pet owner. Bowled over by the cute, cuddly puppy, there is no real notion of the lifetime commitment required to raise the youngster to maturity.

A teen cannot have more than a scant knowledge of the energy demands made on a parent. Her only exposure to little ones may have been baby-sitting. In this setting she has been appreciated and wanted as she is. It is pleasurable to be in charge for a few hours, to be valued as a responsible person.

Why does a teenage girl get pregnant? Often, it happens by virtue of cascading events, one on top of the other, which create a vacuum of existence for her where she does not feel securely loved and valued for just who she is—no matter how irrational or untrue this might actually be. These events can be triggered by the hormonal changes in a girl's body, a lifetime of struggle in a troubled home, or anything in between.

Once a young girl is pregnant, there can be no erasing it. It is time now to gather resources, strength, and understanding in order to make the best of a very difficult situation.

S.O.S. #1

Is your teenager exhibiting any of the following distress signals?

1. Abrupt changes in friends, interests and/or attitudes, which last more than a few days;
2. A sudden drop in the level of her grades, participation in normal activities and/or performance standards at home, school, or work;
3. An outpouring of questions/concerns about subjects such as sex, alcohol/drugs, personal hygiene, or morals;
4. An unusual, lengthy silence/depression;
5. An out-of-the-ordinary desire to spend long periods of time alone.

What Can You Do?

1. Try to talk to the teen about what is bothering her. CAUTION: More listening than talking on your part might be the biggest help. Ask the Lord to bless your efforts.
2. If the teen won't talk, becomes very defensive or storms out of your presence, talk to other adults in her life. Teachers, coaches, employers, and/or parents of close friends can often provide valuable clues about what is going on with your teen.

3. If you still can't gauge the situation but your instincts tell you that something is definitely wrong, follow your instincts! The Holy Spirit is communicating with you. Get to a counselor, psychologist, or pastor and discuss your teen's signals. If the professional agrees that there is trouble brewing, he can hopefully help your teen to open up and begin working on solutions to whatever problems there are.
4. When, somehow, your teen does have the courage to express her problems, bite your tongue and let her get it out! Nothing will send her feelings scurrying back inside faster than your hollering, lecturing, or ridiculing her. Deal with her calmly, as the separate person that she is.

S.O.S. #2

Are any of these alarm bells sounding in your home?

1. A teen breaking curfews that are normally kept;
2. Empty beer cans or liquor bottles in a teen's room, car, or elsewhere;
3. Missing birth control devices from your supply;
4. Hushed telephone conversations between your teen and peers;
5. Unusual overnight/weekend plans supposedly with the girls;
6. Unkempt clothing, make-up, or hair after a date;
7. Abrupt rebellion, depression, or surliness.

What Can You Do?

1. Ask out loud about your concerns—don't just worry,

keeping them to yourself. As a parent, you have an obligation to ask sincere questions and expect reasonable answers.

2. Check out social excursions with other parents. There really is strength in numbers.
3. If yon can't stay awake to greet your teen home from a date, instruct her to wake you. Then look (discreetly) and see if there is an article of clothing inside-out, grass in her hair, an earring missing, etc. (Sometimes the obvious things are her cries for your intervention.)
4. Again, don't hesitate to seek professional help. Professionals work with teens all the time. Don't fear asking for assistance.

S.O.S. #3

Does she know that you love her? If not, she may be asking by:

1. Defiant behavior—trying to determine if you're paying attention. She's asking, "Do you love me enough to notice? Am I important enough for you to discipline me?";
2. Clinging to one of the first few boyfriends she has had—trying to connect with a one-to-one love by going steady. She's begging, "Please take time to love only me sometimes!"
3. Haughtily speaking out about when she has a family of her own—trying to impress upon you that there is something very amiss in her life. She's crying, "I don't have the confidence (or freedom) to tell you some-

thing is wrong, but if you'll only ask me, I will tell you my ideas!"

What Can You Do?

1. Stop a teen when her behavior is unacceptable. To her discipline is an expression of love, which helps her feel secure. How she feels inside can be exactly opposite of how she reacts outwardly.
2. Take the teen in your life out to lunch, shopping, camping, or on a weekend—with just her—where you can take some time to love only her.
3. Ask her what she thinks about parenting, rules, boyfriends, or drugs. If she thinks there's something wrong in her life, then there is. Whether you see it this way or not, the fact is that it is reality to her. Don't necessarily try to be her buddy; she needs guidance much more than endorsement, which means you have to relate to her as a separate person who is not as experienced as you in the ways of the world.
4. Express your love and affection! Tell your teen you love her. Hug her. Take pleasure in her company. Smile at her, laugh with her. If you approve of her, let her know it. Encourage her. Be kind and compassionate toward her. Accept her as a young woman. Pray that, through Christ, God will open the communication lines between you and your teen.

Our Hand in His

Answering the following questions may help adult family members to recognize danger zones in their relationships, which can contribute to a teen pregnancy before it happens; or, to sift through these problem areas and gain an understanding of why if a pregnancy has already happened. The answers can also help a professional attain insight into a family's individual needs.

1. How do you interact with and react to your teen on a daily basis?
2. How do you show your disapproval when she is disobedient or acts inappropriately?
3. How do you show your approval of her when her behavior is appropriate?
4. How do you interact as a family during crises?
5. How do you interact as a family when a member has an outstanding achievement?
6. How do you express love and affection in your family?
7. When you think of your teen, do you have positive, good feelings, or negative, hostile feelings?
8. Is your home environment mostly rushed and tense, or is it usually relaxed and congenial?
9. Are there any extreme, long-term problems in your life, such as financial, marital, or an illness, which might affect how you react toward your teen?
10. Are there unresolved emotional conflicts in your past, such as child abuse, a personal tragedy, or rejection during your own adolescence, which may be hindering your present parenting skills?
11. Does your family accept change with an optimistic, *rolling* attitude, or one of dread and fear?
12. How easily swayed is your family by circumstance, mood, or others' presence?
13. How consistent are your beliefs, values, rules, and/or standards?
14. How do you feel about sex?
15. Do you talk about sex in your home?

16. Are you sensitive to changes in the moods of family members, including your teen?
17. Do you drink alcohol, smoke marijuana, or otherwise use drugs recreationally?
18. How is the subject of these substances handled in your family?
19. Are there pressures that involve serious crippling effects, such as alcoholism, physical and/or mental abuse, sexual deviations (incest, homosexuality, etc.), severe poverty, or the adverse effects of a divorce in your home?
20. Are you generally an approachable, open person, or a reserved, structured individual?

CHAPTER TWO

So, Now She's Pregnant

Sheri had dated Greg for a year when she found out she was pregnant. For several days now, she has existed in a trancelike state, going through her regular motions at home, school, and on dates. She hasn't told anyone of her pregnancy, not even Greg.

Sitting at her desk, Sheri looks up at her bulletin board. There are ribbons from speech contests, cheerleading camp, and softball tournaments. There are photos of her older sister's two children, and several friends, including one of Greg—bits and pieces of her life as a sophomore in high school.

Sheri puts her head in her hands and sobs. She feels so guilty as if she has murdered someone! But, then, to her parents, it would probably seem as though she has killed a part of them. Oh, how could she have gotten herself into this mess? How could it ever work out? Sheri feels she has ruined her life.

Lara and Neil were celebrating Christmas break from school the night they first made love. Lara had gone to a

Family Planning Clinic before classes started in the fall and gotten birth control pills. A counselor there had been pleasant, and spent several minutes talking to her about sexual relationships, birth control, disease, and being responsible. However, she had only half-listened, having already made up her mind to enjoy her last year of high school as a contemporary, sexually active woman, even though her parents had stressed the importance of abstinence during her growing-up years.

Lara had trouble remembering to take her pill each day. It was hard because she had to hide them away so that her parents wouldn't find them. Since she was very busy, she would forget once in a while. But she felt safe because the next day she would just take two pills.

Unfortunately, three weeks before her graduation, Lara found out she was pregnant. She didn't tell her parents. Neither of them had had the opportunity to pursue a higher education, and they had scrimped and saved all of Lara's life so that she and her younger sister could go to college. Now, Lara would disappoint them terribly.

The day of her commencement, Lara could not look her parents in the eyes, she was so ashamed of what she knew she must soon tell them. Each time a relative came to congratulate her or she overheard a proud comment about her from her father, she winced with regret.

Marcy started her period when she was 13. She began going to movies and dances with Eric the same year—seventh grade. The two called each other on the telephone every night. They passed love notes throughout the day at school. Marcy's parents had been divorced two years before, and she deeply resented the upheaval in her life.

Eric was very insecure. He wanted everyone to like

him and he would do just about anything to gain his peers' approval. This included going all the way with Marcy.

The two coupled, more in a blind pursuit of healing their separate inner pains than anything else. Their minds and hearts were not mature enough to deal with what their bodies could physically accomplish.

Marcy was pregnant less than halfway into her first year of junior high school. However, she was so naive about the physical symptoms that, until she could no longer button her pants at four months pregnant, she did not realize anything was amiss.

The panic that filled Marcy as the doctor told her and her mother that she was pregnant was so consuming that Marcy shook uncontrollably for several minutes. She had to lie back on the examining table, listening to her mother's gasping questions, and only partly hearing the doctor's matter-of-fact answers.

Sheri, Lara, and Marcy each got pregnant under very different circumstances. But their feelings of guilt, shame, and fear are universal to all pregnant teens. Add to these confusion, and there is so much anxiety that teens can be totally consumed. These girls experience an inner loneliness that is so pervasive it physically hurts.

BREAKING THE NEWS

To cover up her feelings of loneliness and anxiety, Jessica erected a facade of elation about her pregnancy at 16. Ryan, her boyfriend of two years, was the father of the baby. Rather than give in to her despair, Jessica twisted her mood into one of joy. The evening after she found out she was pregnant, she told Ryan the news with a wide grin on her face, as though she had won a much-desired prize.

Ryan reacted by following her lead—told her he loved her, that if she was happy so was he and, of course, he would marry her.

The second evening after discovering the pregnancy, Ryan arrived at Jessica's home with shaking hands. The pair wold tell Jessica's parents, Al and Betty, about the situation. The four were sitting in the family room watching television when Jessica's voice rang out merrily, "Mom, Dad, Ryan and I have something to tell you."

Both adults looked at their daughter, Al with slight annoyance at being interrupted, and Betty with wariness.

"Well," Jessica beamed at Ryan, "we have some good news and some bad news."

She faltered only seconds before continuing, "The bad news is—I'm pregnant. The good news is we're getting married!"

Shock, Pain and Anger

Al exploded out of his chair. "Like hell you are!" He looked at Jessica, then to his wife. "What is she saying? Did you know about this?"

Betty's face was white. "Of course not! Jessica, this is not funny, but I hope it's a joke."

"No, it's not a joke." Jessica's bravado began to fail her as she saw the effect the news was having on her parents. She looked at Ryan. He sat with his hands on his knees, looking down at the floor. She quickly turned back to her mother. However, Jessica's pleading eyes met a cloud of hurt so dense she couldn't penetrate it at all. Her mother had sunk deep in her chair, and looked very small. There was no help there.

Jessica darted a look toward her father, who stood with his fists clenched at his sides, his face an angry red. "I can't believe you would do this to us!" he shouted.

"I—" Jessica started to stammer, but her father raised an arm as if to ward off a blow. He looked at Ryan.

"And you!" he spat. "How could you do such a thing to my daughter? You disgusting little brat! Get out of my house and don't let me see you here again!"

Ryan's head snapped up and he looked very frightened. "Jessica, I think I'd better go now. We'll talk about this later."

"Oh, no, we won't!" Al advanced a step toward Ryan, then checked himself. "Just get out of here, boy!"

Ryan looked helplessly at Jessica, then left in defeat. Jessica sat frozen in her spot. Any pretense of gladness was gone, and in its place was fear.

Placing the Blame

Al turned on Betty. "You!" he roared. "This is your fault! If you hadn't been so lenient with her—letting her go out with that kid so long! Didn't I tell you there would be trouble?"

Betty finally sparked to life. "Me? You hypocrite! If you hadn't been so strict with her—always pushing her away from us with your rules and criticism!"

Before her eyes, Jessica saw her parents take their rage out on each other for the first time in her life. When she could stand it no longer, she fled the room in tears. There was little sleep in the house that night. Each one—father, mother and daughter—lay awake in his or her own torment.

Al stared out the bedroom window most of the night, filled with resentment toward Jessica, his wife and the young boy Ryan. He felt totally powerless. All those years of raising his family, working to provide a good home and opportunities for his children! His two older sons were in college and doing fine. He was proud of them. Jessica, the apple of his eye, had been such a pleasure to him. Sure, he had always kept a close eye on her, but only because he loved her so much. He had wanted the best for his little girl.

Now, repulsed at the thought of her entangled in this boy's arms, he was disgusted by the very image of her in

As parents, your responsibility is to try to bear with your child in her time of greatest need.

his mind. How could she? Her mother should have seen this coming!

Betty lay awake in the darkness, only feet away from her husband. Hot streams of silent tears ran from the sides of her eyes, across her temples, and down into her hair. A heavy disappointment squeezed her so tightly that she felt as though her heart would burst from the pressure of it.

"Oh, Jessica, what were you thinking?" she said to herself. "Whatever was in your mind to let this happen?"

Overwhelmed, Betty prayed silently, "Father how could you let my daughter get pregnant? She's only a child! Why didn't you protect her? She's too young to be a parent! Too young to be held responsible for her actions!"

Several statements made by their pastor at a recent seminar on drugs, sex and raising teenagers popped into Betty's mind. "God is not a super-cop. He does not wait behind a billboard at the side of the road to catch your child before she speeds on to tragedy.

"He has given us all free will, including your teenager. If she chooses to slip into the fast lane of sin, then she does so outside the umbrella of His blessing.

"She must then live with the consequences of her actions. As parents, your responsibility is to try to bear with your child in her time of greatest need. When she has made a poor choice, you must try to love her with compassion and patient guidance. As difficult as it might be, try to forgive her as God forgives each of you."

Betty tried to let her mind settle on these thoughts and wondered, as she prayed very hard, if she had the strength to see her daughter through all that was to come.

Jessica sat on her bed, rocking back and forth, wishing throughout the long night that she could turn back the clock.

In the morning, Al and Betty, looking haggard, sat with their coffee as Jessica walked quietly into the room. She felt so miserable she couldn't speak. When she tried to have some cereal, she couldn't eat.

Finally, Jessica gave up and left the room. She heard her mother start to cry. She'd give anything to take back her pregnancy, to never have made love with Ryan at all—but it was too late.

Betty went to busy herself with dishes at the sink. She watched the hummingbirds at the feeder and wondered where she had gone wrong. What could she have done to prevent this horrible situation?

Al wrestled with his own guilt. He went to the garage and tinkered with the mower. His thoughts, tangled even more now with feeling that he had failed his daughter, ran a desperate course from anger, to resentment, to hurt, and back to guilt.

It was a bright Sunday morning, but the darkness in their home penetrated every corner.

Living with Tension

On Monday, Jessica went to school, and her parents each went to their respective jobs. Betty, a loan officer at a local bank, sat at her desk answering the usual number of phone calls and questions. Her feelings were not usual, though. Every time she talked with co-workers, she wondered what they would think when they found out about Jessica. In her mind, she knew she shouldn't be concerned about what others thought but, in her heart, she felt ashamed.

Al, a realtor, was deeply affected by anticipating what others might think of his allowing his daughter to get so out of control that she got pregnant. He hadn't protected her, and now he thought he would be publicly humiliated. The whole family would be disgraced!

The next several days were very strained in their household. Jessica talked to Ryan at school, mainly about how her parents were reacting. The couple decided it was best not to tell Ryan's parents until hers had settled down. Jessica was more guarded with Ryan than usual. She was disappointed that Ryan had slunk away when her father had yelled at him. Inside, she wished he would have been more aggressive, that he would have defended her. She was carrying his baby—he needed to be a man now.

For his part, Ryan was extremely confused. He had been completely surprised at Jessica's announcement that she was pregnant because he had assumed she would take any necessary precautions against such a thing. Also, her joyful reaction had been an even bigger shock. He had let himself be swept into the mood, but then, with Jessica's father's explosion, Ryan had come back to earth with a thud. And now, he didn't know what to do.

Jessica's parents, also confused, maintained a silence between them as they struggled with their separate feelings. When their daughter was in the same room, there was an uncomfortable tension that enveloped the three.

Regrouping

Betty began a regrouping of her emotions first. The reality of the pregnancy started to sink in and, with it, came immediate fears of all sorts. Jessica's health—could she carry the baby? Would the baby be normal? What should they do? She could not imagine her daughter being married! She was absolutely against abortions. But could she force her daughter to give the baby up for adoption? Did she want to? She doubted she could live with giving her own grandchild away.

Betty also felt a small amount of optimism about becoming a grandmother. This completely surprised her, and she felt guilty for being even a tiny bit excited by the thought of Jessica, as a teenager, bringing a child into their lives.

But accepting this as a seed of hope, she finally approached Al. "You know, it won't do any good for us to keep blaming each other, or to avoid discussing Jessica's pregnancy.

"She's going to be pregnant whether we talk about it or not. We've got too many years invested in keeping this family together to let us be torn apart now, Al."

Her husband looked across the table at his wife. The pain in his eyes tore at her heart. His bottom lip trembled and, letting go of the grief he had held inside all these days, he put his head in his hands and wept.

Betty quickly rose and went around the table to him. She gathered him in her arms and gently whispered, "It'll be okay. We'll get through this. I know we will. I don't know how, but we will."

When Al's emotions were spent, he reached up to clasp Betty's hands. "I just feel so helpless. I don't know what to do."

"Well," Betty said, hoping some humor might lessen the pain, "you could look at the bright side—you'll get a head start on being a grandpa!"

"Oooh!" Al groaned, "just what I need to hear!"

"Oh, Al, it won't help at all to torture ourselves with bitterness. I guess we just need to dig in and do whatever has to be done."

THE BABY'S FATHER AND HIS PARENTS

Ryan couldn't take the pressure any longer. He broke down in front of his mother after school the same day that Al and Betty talked. He told her about Jessica's pregnancy. Marie Lang looked at her son and said, simply, "Oh, Ryan, no."

She sat down at the table for several minutes in a daze. Ryan finally broke the silence. "Mom! Say something!"

"I don't know what to say, Ryan. What can I say? You're 16 years old—a junior in high school! Do you want me to congratulate you?"

"No, Mom." Ryan shook his head sadly. "I don't care—hit me, cuss at me, just something!"

"Oh, Ryan!" Marie looked at her son compassionately. "What good will any of those things do? I need some time to think. I can't imagine what your dad's going to say."

"Who cares!" Ryan responded bitterly. "He's never around any other time. Why should he be now?"

Paul and Marie Lang had been divorced for nine years. Paul's job took him away from town during the week and he was quite often busy socially on the weekends. There was much dissension between Ryan and Paul. Ryan held an extreme grudge against his father for not paying more attention to him.

"Ryan," Marie said flatly, "don't be so harsh about your dad. We've been over this a thousand times. He's a busy man."

Ryan's two younger sisters were 13 and 14 respectively. Ryan had felt a lot of responsibility in the household since his parents' split, which complicated his feelings about Jessica's pregnancy even more. What would his mother and sisters do without his help? The weight he felt on his shoulders was great.

Marie looked at her son with sorrow. What would they do? Ryan had no more experience earning money than neighborhood lawn mowing jobs. How would he ever support a family? There was no question of options in Marie's mind. She had been 16, also, when she had become pregnant with Ryan and, of course, she and Paul had been married. For the moment, Marie didn't consider any other possibility.

Her thoughts turned more toward how to make it happen financially now, and how the couple might fare in the future. She and Paul had stuck it out for seven years before their divorce. Though she was upset about Ryan and Jessica, it didn't really shock her. After two years together, Marie thought they were bound to be involved. She regretted not having talked to Ryan about birth control, but what was done was done. Her son was responsible.

Ryan was very mature for his age and a sensitive boy. He would be good to Jessica and their child. But how would he support them? Ryan really had no specific career ambitions. And if he didn't finish high school, what chance would he have at a decent job? Maybe Paul would have some answers.

Paul, however, was not quite so coolheaded about the situation. He hollered at Ryan and at Marie. There was a horrible scene in front of their daughters, and Paul ended up leaving with a final threat. "I wash my hands of it! If you people don't see that getting that girl an abortion is the only answer, then I won't have any more to do with it!"

Marie heaved a sigh of painful resignation. "Ryan, it may take your dad a while to cool down. I should have known he would be more upset about this then I was."

"When we had to get married at your age, it was quite a blow to him. He had high hopes for playing football at college, and blamed his parents for not helping us out with money so that he could still go.

"That's why your dad's always driven himself so hard at work—to prove to himself and to his parents that he could succeed on his own. One of his main goals in life has been to give you kids the kind of start he felt he never had."

"Great," Ryan muttered, "now he's going to blame me for ruining his life—again."

"No, Ryan!" Marie answered quickly. "I didn't mean it that way! Paul has loved you children more than anything! I'm only trying to explain why he feels so upset."

Ryan shrugged. "So? Your marriage broke up. He's never around. Now he hates me! Why should I care why?"

"No! He doesn't hate you!" Marie realized, too late, what a wound she had opened up. Here was her son, at his most vulnerable, under a mountainous burden that would indeed change the course of his entire life, and now she had led him to feel responsible for repeating a painful family history.

"Ryan, listen to me." Marie forced a calm tone into her voice. "Nobody's life has been ruined. Your dad and I were too young to get married and start a family. You and Jessica are, too. But you are also completely different people than we were. If we can all pull together now and give you kids the best possible start, maybe you'll make it."

"Wait a minute." Ryan looked confused. "Are you saying you want me to get married?"

"Well, of course." Marie looked back at Ryan with surprise. "You're responsible for the life of a child. You have to live up to that responsibility!"

Ryan turned white. He clenched his fists on top of the table. "First, Jessica expects me to be happy she's pregnant. Then, I'm forced to feel like a whipped dog in front of her father. Now, you tell me I have to get married! And Dad says Jessica should get an abortion! Well, just maybe, I feel trapped! I'd like to know if anybody's gonna ask me what I feel or want?"

Marie looked into her lap, tears springing to her eyes. "Ryan," she said quietly, "you should have thought of that before."

TEAMWORK IS IMPERATIVE

Two evenings later, Marie was sitting nervously at a table with Jessica's parents, in their home. Al was fidgeting with his wedding ring. Betty was trying to make small talk. The three waited for Jessica and Ryan to join them.

"Marie," Betty ventured, "have you thought about what you feel should be done?"

"Well," Marie said softly, "my feeling is that there is only one thing to do. They should get married."

"I see." Betty sounded noncommittal. She neither agreed nor disagreed. It struck her that the most difficult part of this situation, for now, would be mixing ideas, values, and feelings in order to come out with a course of action that was satisfactory to everyone. Ryan, Jessica,

Al, Betty, and Marie would each have their own thoughts; Jessica had hysterically related that Ryan's father wanted her to have an abortion. It sounded as if they might be in for some rough going.

Relative strangers before this, the adults must now discuss several very delicate and intimate subjects in helping two children sort through the issues that would catapult them into adulthood. A huge challenge for one family, Betty thought, but to solve the problems with two families' input would be a miracle!

Ryan and Jessica came to the table and sat down. Everyone poised on the edges of their chairs, waiting for someone to break the silence.

Al was the first to speak. "Well, we better start talking. Looks like we're going to be thrown together pretty close, so we might as well try and relax."

"Yes," Marie added, "why don't you tell us how you feel, Jessica?" Marie felt a twinge of helplessness. She knew that it was Jessica's body, and that the girl would be the one to carry and deliver a child. She also knew that, even though times had changed, the main responsibilities of daily parenting still fell largely on mothers. As Ryan's mother, Marie didn't know that she would have as much to say about what would be done, and it made her feel somewhat threatened. Half of her was glad Paul had refused to come this night, for fear he would have become irrational, but the other half of her desperately wished for a supportive teammate.

Jessica's voice, in answer to Marie's suggestion, shook as she began. "Well, I, uh . . . oh, I don't know," she trailed off in exasperation, but Betty gently covered her daughter's hand with her own.

"It's okay, honey," she reassured her. "Take your time and be honest. That's why we're here together. We need to let each other know how we feel and deal with it as best we can."

"All right," Jessica went on. "It's just that everyone seems to think that because we're young, we're dumb. I feel like we aren't going to be allowed to make any decisions."

"Jessica," Al cut in, "I don't think you'd better worry about what you think we feel or want. I think you better let us tell you ourselves."

Betty lay a cautioning hand on Al's shoulder. "Jessica, we want to know what you feel about being pregnant and what you hope to do from here."

Jessica nodded. "I am happy I'm going to have a baby," she said bravely. "And I hope Ryan and I will get married.

"I know it's hard for you guys to understand, but we have been together for two years. I know we're young, but we do love each other and want to make our life together."

Jessica looked at Ryan with a hopeful expression, silently pleading that he felt the same way.

"Ryan," Betty turned to him, "how do you feel about becoming a father and, maybe, a husband?"

Ryan hesitated several seconds. "I guess, mixed up. I do love Jessica," he said, "but, I'm nervous, too. A wife and a baby—that's a big decision."

"A little late to realize that now!" Al said gruffly. "You get my daughter pregnant, and then say you're not sure you want to marry her?"

"Al," Betty quickly broke in, "Ryan has a right to his feelings, just like you do. We can't start name-calling or blaming here. We have to stay level-headed."

Marie thought she was deeply in debt to Betty for the woman's calm but firm leadership. It was imperative that they all work toward the same goal—what was best for the kids, including the unborn child.

Al shrugged his shoulders and clasped his hands in front of him on the table. "Okay. Go ahead, boy."

Where had the tender, loving boy who had been so close to her a few weeks ago gone? In his place was a scared teenager who wasn't sure of himself or their future.

"I don't mean to upset you, sir," Ryan said, acknowledging Al's concern. "And I realize a big mistake has been made here. But I feel like I have to say what I think now, so I don't make any more.

"I do love Jessica. But I don't know if I can support us. I don't know where I can get a job, or how we'll finish school. I'm just mixed up!"

Jessica's stomach was full of butterflies. She thought she was hearing things. Where had the tender, loving boy who had been so close to her a few weeks ago gone? In his place was a scared teenager who wasn't sure of himself or their future.

Betty watched the play of panic across her daughter's face. Her heart ached for her, and she breathed a silent prayer for Jessica to be strengthened.

Aloud she said, "I think you both have good reason to be confused. But if we all respect each other's feelings and join together in working this out, I think we can keep it in perspective."

Al looked at the other four and wondered if they'd ever be able to work through all the issues at hand as a group. He hated the thought of losing his daughter to a young boy who probably couldn't take care of her, much less take care of a child.

They each talked more, in turn, about how they felt about the pregnancy. As emotions were shaky, they decided to call it an early night and discuss the situation further another time. Betty quietly suggested they all join hands, and she prayed aloud, thanking God for His blessings, asking for His wisdom in sorting out their problems, and for forgiveness of their sins.

DEALING WITH THE REACTIONS OF OTHERS

As the news spread at school about Jessica's pregnancy, there came advice from many corners. Several teachers expressed their concern, and each had an idea about what should be done. There was a resounding consensus that she and Ryan should finish high school. Jessica tried hard to listen politely, take in what seemed useful, and pay no attention to those ideas that were not appropriate to her situation. She held onto the fact that, as her mother had said, the decision rested within the families. Nobody else had to live with it.

Jessica's girlfriends glamourized the circumstance. They were dreamy-eyed over her having a baby, setting up house, being with a man to love every day, and being independent. They immediately began to plan a personal shower for her, even though a decision to get married had not been made.

When Jessica told her mother about the shower Betty said, "That's very nice, dear. But, remember, they aren't in your shoes. Don't be carried away by the idealistic part of this and lose sight of reality. That might put each of us on different sides of a fence, and things will be that much tougher to work out."

"I won't, Mom," Jessica answered, "but I need to enjoy the things I can about all this. I can't walk around serious and mopey all the time. That won't change things!"

"Well, Jess, it is serious." Betty used her daughter's pet name for the first time since finding out she was pregnant. "You have to keep down to earth and take one step at a time."

The doorbell rang. Jessica went to answer it, and there stood her grandmother.

"Gram!" Jessica squealed, "what are you doing here? Mom didn't tell me you were coming!"

Betty's mother held out her arms to hug Jessica. "Well, from the sound of things, you could use some help around here!"

Jessica stiffened in her grandmother's arms. "You know?"

"It's okay, darling. I'm not here to get after you—only to love you up a little."

Unbidden tears stung Jessica's eyes. "Oh, Gram! I'm so scared," she sobbed.

"I know, baby, I know."

Betty came up behind Jessica, and put her arms around her daughter and her mother. "Hi, Mom" was all she said. The three had a long cry together and, with cleansed spirits, they sat down for a warm visit.

Betty had telephoned her mother several days earlier, fearing that the older woman would be terribly shocked to learn that her only granddaughter was pregnant at 16. But with the wisdom of age, grandma wasn't nearly so upset.

She had been very philosophical about the Lord working in mysterious ways and things turning out for the best. Grandma had offered to come from her home three hours away for a few days to help her family, if she could.

This had been of great comfort to Betty, especially after Al's mother, who, thankfully, lived several hundred miles away, screamed at Betty over the phone that she and Al hadn't protected Jessica from the boy she was sure was no more than a sex fiend.

For the pregnant girl, one of the biggest challenges she may often face is to forgive herself.

WHERE TO GO FOR HELP

Nearly a week later after many discussions, nothing definite had been decided. Betty finally suggested to everyone that they seek professional help. She had called their pastor, who said he would be happy to counsel everyone involved.

Jessica felt more comfortable with the idea of going to the family's doctor, who was also willing to help them.

Marie wondered if a marriage and family therapist or a family planning expert might be better trained to counsel them.

One of Al's clients was a psychologist, and seemed a reliable source of help.

In fact, any of these mentioned are sound, valuable sources of assistance during a time of crisis. Professionals can be objective about the issues facing those involved. They can help to bring out volatile feelings in an acceptable manner, and present questions that may be too hard for family members to confront on their own.

For the pregnant girl, one of the biggest challenges she may often face is to forgive herself. Her conscience is paining her greatly. During this time, she is very weak. Hopefully, those who love her will rush to form a support network around her, and professional guidance can be an important part of this network's strength.

And the greatest Counselor of all, the Holy Spirit, will be with her. He grieves with the teenage girl who is pregnant. He suffers with her and wants to guide her in her time of need.

A teen pregnancy does not have to be the ruination of anyone's life. It can be a time of tremendous growth in faith, hope, and love. James 1:12 says: *Blessed is the man who perseveres under trial, because when he has stood the test, he will receive the crown of life that God has promised to those who love him.*

Certainly, dealing with a teenage pregnancy is an intense trial but, with God's help, all things are surmountable.

A last note in preparation to explore the options available to pregnant teens and their families: Go gently, friends; for every teen parent, there will most likely be a teenage son or daughter in 13 years, wondering if he or she was a devastating influence on his or her parents' lives. What is done now will have effects on that child, too!

S.O.S. #4

Is there a pregnant teenager in your life? If so, she may be:

1. Feeling she has ruined her own, and other peoples' lives;

2. Frightened and confused, sometimes to the point of hysteria;
3. Ashamed to such a degree that, in order to cope, she may be twisting her reaction to her pregnancy into one of elation, or giving in to total despair;
4. Experiencing a guilt so intense that all she may be able to consider is finding a way out of her situation. Beware of instability that indicates a teen might do something desperate, such as getting an abortion, attempting a self-inflicted abortion, running away, or committing suicide.

   Such indications may include: unusual and/or morbid questions about death; extreme depression; a manic pretense of joy over her pregnancy; sudden concern over and/or disappearance of money; and/or anything that causes you to feel uneasy about the way she is coping.

What Can You Do?

1. Assert that the foremost thing is the teen's safety. Your feelings, reactions, options, and ways of coping can be dealt with one at a time, but do whatever has to be done to keep her from harm. If you are a distraught parent suffering your own pain and you don't feel able to discuss the emotions that are tearing your daughter apart—get help!

   Take her to a professional, ask another trusted adult to talk with her, have her stay with relatives/friends for a few days, or otherwise keep her in the presence of a responsible adult as much as possible.
2. If you do feel capable of calmly dealing with the teen, then reinforce the fact that nothing is so bad it can't be handled. Stress the importance of letting some time

pass before taking any action in regard to the pregnancy.

3. Point out to the teen that millions of girls before her have survived teen pregnancies, and many more will after her. Emphasize that she is not alone and, with God's help, you will work through the problems together.
4. Hold hands and pray together. If you are not comfortable praying aloud, each do so silently. Ask God to give you the answers and wisdom you need to do His will during this time. Ask Him to forgive your sins and thank Him for this opportunity to grow in your faith and lives as His children.

   Remember Jesus' promise in John 14:18: *I will not leave you as orphans; I will come to you.*
5. Refer to Colossians 3:12-14: *Therefore, as God's chosen people, holy and dearly loved, clothe yourselves with compassion, kindness, humility, gentleness and patience. Bear with each other and forgive whatever grievances you may have against one another. Forgive as the Lord forgave you. And over all these virtues put on love, which binds them all together in perfect unity.*

S.O.S. #5

How do you feel about your teen's pregnancy?

1. Angry?
2. Resentful, blameful, disgusted?
3. Guilty?
4. Ashamed?
5. Disappointed?
6. Fearful, anxious and/or overwhelmed?

7. Sad, mournful?
8. Even a tiny bit hopeful, excited?

What Can You Do?

1. Realize that perfectly normal, loving parents can feel enraged over the news that their teen is pregnant. Try to deal with this anger as constructively as you can. Work through it so that the healing process can begin. Some ways of doing this might be to direct your energy into (or toward) other objects—clean the garage, dig in the garden, wash the car, beat the patio with a broom—anything that won't harm you, or another person. Ephesians 4:31 tells us: **Get rid of all bitterness, rage and anger, brawling and slander, along with every form of malice.**
2. Don't expect too much of yourself. Let your emotions take their natural course. Often, as a coping mechanism to the shock and magnitude of the pregnancy, parents initially try to place the responsibility of it onto one another, the father of the baby, his parents, society, peers, even God! A pregnancy brings the abrupt end of a teenager's life as it is known to those close to her—a passing away of the familiar, and an immediate change in dealing with her life. With this shock, comes grief. Try to express this grief—cry, pray, share it with others, read information on the subject, but try not to direct your feelings at those close to you.
3. Turn to God. In John 14:1 Jesus says: *Do not let your hearts be troubled. Trust in God; trust also in me.* Painful feelings are a part of our existence. But He is there, waiting for us to let Him help.
4. Guilt is a near useless emotion. It is associated with

what has already happened. For example, who feels guilty over the angry words he might speak next year? Guilt is only productive when it provides the initiative for positive change. It is imperative that those involved with a pregnant teen realize that the contributions each may or may not have made to why she got pregnant will not change the existing condition. Therefore, if there are problems in this area to work out, they can be taken care of later.

For now, let go of your guilt, so that you can be an effective help in doing what's best for your teen. Resolve that when the immediate crises have passed and decisions about her pregnancy have been made, you will sit down with her and/or professional help, and talk about the role you may have played in her getting pregnant. Then you can begin to work through any residual effects.

5. If you are experiencing more than fleeting moments of shame, and a feeling of total disgrace is sticking with you over your teen's pregnancy, try to realize that this is not the time to think of what others think of you, your family and especially the teen. Read Romans 10:11: *As the Scripture says, "Anyone who trusts in him will never be put to shame.*
6. For all the uncomfortable reactions to a teen pregnancy—fear, anxiety, disgust, anger, resentment, and guilt—there is a tried and true formula for surviving: (1) Accept the fact that, yes, this is happening to you! (2) Face the issues at hand and do what needs to be done; for instance, make a doctor's appointment, talk to the school principal, buy your daughter a book on pregnancy, etc., and (3) Let tomorrow come—time will pass. The grocery store will still sell food, the mail will still arrive, and there

will still be birds singing all the while your daughter is pregnant. Let it happen, and with each new day you will adjust a little more, understand a little better, and feel a little more optimistic.

7. Coming together after several days or weeks of terrific strain can be an extremely fulfilling experience. There is hardly a more poignant demonstration of love's driving power than a coming together of what has been separated! Don't hinder the process. You have no obligation to stay mad at or punish your daughter. She needs your unconditional love and concern. Pray that God will help you have the strength to give it to her. First Peter 4:8 tells us: *Above all, love each other deeply, because love covers over a multitude of sins.*

S.O.S. #6

As a teammate with your daughter, spouse, the father of her baby, his parents, and/or any professional caregiver involved, are you giving your best team-play effort?

What Can You Do?

1. Remember that *what you say can, and will, be used against you.* It is impossible to bring forth any good team effort if one or more players is spewing out nasty names, calling unjust blames, pouting, acting self-righteous, or being disagreeable on offered suggestions from other teammates. Further, words do break, if not bones, hearts. They can scar relationships for a long time.
2. Normally, a successful team is comprised of a group

that has practiced a particular activity for many weeks or months together. However, unlike a baseball game or theatrical performance, a teen pregnancy draws its team members into play abruptly, often not having previously known each other well at all. Understandably, this can feel quite strange and, at times, downright uncomfortable.

Try to be like a chosen member of an All-Star Team that does not usually have a large amount of time to practice together, but rather shines forth, rising to the occasion, and giving the effort its all. Bear in mind that, in the case of teen pregnancy, there are no trophies; there are only human lives for whom you are striving to succeed.

3. The *Good-Old-Boy* network has traditionally consisted of individuals who, collectively, have many things in common. Their team may be made up of businessmen who all, seemingly, share the same tips, athletic clubs, and restaurants.

   You may not be so lucky with the father of your teen's baby, or his family. There may be great differences in your beliefs, values, status, and life-styles. And it may be very difficult to blend these. A good team member is one who knows that respect for other peoples' rights to their own opinions is essential.
4. Often, unpredictable emotions can rise up at the least convenient moments. If a team is fighting one another on the football field, it is imperative that a time-out be called. Likewise, if your daughter's boyfriend starts railing at his father for all the times he wished Dad would have told him he loved him, then time-out should be called. Back off when emotions get eruptive.
5. Remember that a good teammate is a good sport. A

sense of perspective and humor goes a long way in accomplishing this.

6. Do not pull any sneak plays! They tend to backfire and can humiliate your fellow teammates. Uncle Harry, the preacher from out of town, should not just happen to drop in the night you are meeting with the whole team. If Uncle Harry is there, it should only be because all have agreed that he should be.
7. Do not look at the situation as if it is *your* team and *their* team. The boy's family and yours are one team fighting for the future of your children, and their child.

Our Hand in His

Answering the following questions may help you gain a healthy perspective on the reactions you, your teen, and/or others closely involved may have to the teen pregnancy. Also, your answers to these questions can help a professional caregiver spot any problem areas before they get out of hand.

1. Read James 5:16. It says: *Therefore confess your sins to each other and pray for each other so that you may be healed. The prayer of a righteous man is powerful and effective.*
2. Are you letting self-pity, disappointment, resentment, or other negative feelings get in the way of positive communication?
3. Have you accepted the reality of the situation, and gone beyond trying to think of a way out?
4. Are you really trusting God? Or are you saying that you are, and then continuing to fret, worry, push for answers, trying to control parts of the circumstances that are not yours to control?

5. Have you accepted that it is all right to feel hope and optimism about the future, even in a seemingly devastating situation?
6. Have you accepted negative emotions are normal?
7. Are you holding back the process of healing by assuming a position of punishing your daughter for what she has supposedly done to you?
8. Have you let feelings of shame/disgrace get too big a hold on you?
9. Are you letting tomorrow come, or are you trying to push too fast?
10. Are you allowing love to enter your heart and aid in your family's healing?
11. Are you being a supportive, contributing team member with the others involved in your teen's pregnancy?
12. Are you being careful with the words you speak, expressions you wear, and reactions you have?
13. Are you overcoming the uncomfortableness of possibly having been thrown into a team of strangers?
14. Have you confronted the depth and importance of making decisions that affect an unborn child of God?
15. Are you being tolerant and accepting of the other peoples' feelings?
16. Are you respecting others (and yourself) by calling a time-out when emotions are overwhelming?
17. Have you vowed to be a teammate on one team, or have you separated into two: Your Family and Their Family?
18. Have you considered Ephesians 4:32? It says: *Be kind and compassionate to one another, forgiving each other, just as in Christ God forgave you.*

CHAPTER THREE

What Are Her Options?

When Angie got pregnant at 14, her father's initial reaction about what to do was quick in coming: "She's got to get married!"

Cara's mother's was just as fast. "You're only 15! There's no choice but to give the baby up for adoption!"

When a teenage daughter comes home pregnant, emotions can be so colored that, at first, there appears to be only one way out. However, this is rarely the case. There are normally several options to consider and, as time passes, things will settle down a bit and these options can be examined. It is absolutely essential that decisions not be made too hastily. The pregnancy will not disappear, and all parties involved will be affected, regardless of what course of action is followed.

THE CHOICE IS FOR A LIFETIME

Heather's parents were so sure they knew the best thing

for her was to keep her baby but remain single and live at home with them that they railroaded her into a corner. They wouldn't listen to her or let her express her feelings at all. Heather became so frustrated that she ran away with her boyfriend and, supposedly, got married by a so-called minister in a large city. The bedraggled pair returned home several days later when their money ran out.

This infuriated the domineering parents even more, and they pushed Heather so hard that she and her boyfriend/husband ended up living with his parents for the duration of Heather's pregnancy. When a beautiful son was born to her, Heather refused to see her parents or allow them to visit. The family's sad relationship has never mended.

Helpless though a parent of a pregnant teen may feel, it will benefit no one to try and force an issue. The teen has feelings and rights. She is in need of guidance to make decisions, not in need of having them made for her.

As Nancy's parents, who communicated fairly well with her, prepared to help her with making decisions about her pregnancy, they sorted through their own feelings first. Hal and Alecia Morgan had five children. Nancy was in the middle, with a younger sister and brother at home, and two older brothers, both married with their own families.

Alecia feared that Nancy's pregnancy at 16 resulted from Nancy's not having received the attention she needed to feel secure; and, being torn between other siblings' needs, she had sought another to provide this security. However, it had already been established that the boyfriend would have nothing to do with the situation now.

Hal agreed that Nancy's pregnancy might be a subconscious cry for attention. He also strongly advocated, for several legitimate reasons, that Nancy's baby be given up for adoption.

One was that he didn't think Nancy's personality was geared toward the extreme adjustments required by motherhood. He felt as if her own great need for security would be done a deep injustice by pushing her into parenthood.

Alecia, in turn, agreed with her husband about Nancy's personality, but didn't think she could see their grandchild "given away." She felt that if Nancy had her baby and lived with them, they could help raise the baby.

Hal was not at all sure they had that much to give to another child, emotionally. He had been looking forward to the time in their lives when he and Alecia could spend more time alone together. He did not relish the thought of starting all over again with a new child, not to mention the added complications of the baby actually being their grandchild.

Financially, Hal also had doubts about making an additional lifetime commitment. Another child to raise meant money required that might otherwise be needed for college tuitions for their younger kids, security for him and Alecia in their retirement years, etc. He wasn't thinking in terms of selfish luxuries, but real obligations that were already foreseeable.

True, Nancy wouldn't necessarily be with them forever, but there were no guarantees; and having a child with them from birth, knowing that the two would most likely leave someday, presented its own set of anxieties and problems.

One of Alecia's few concerns about taking on the responsibilities of helping to raise a grandchild had to do with her and Hal's ages. Over 50, they no longer had the physical energy nor the level of patience they had when raising their five children. They were more set in their ways now, less flexible.

Each of these considerations is a bona fide item for parents to go over in deciding what they can or cannot give to their teen daughter who is pregnant. Choosing the best option with and for her involves honest evaluation of the emotional, financial, and physical resources available to the family.

In conjunction with the teen's own personality and her adaptive potential, choices may become easier to make.

TALK! TALK! TALK!

The best tool available in working toward the right direction for the pregnant teen is talking. There is no amount of talk that can be too much. Even simple conversations about everyday things can yield valuable clues as to the teen's inner feelings and desires, things she may be unable to define and/or express during intense discussions about her situation directly.

Susan's feelings are quite common. She and her family, along with her boyfriend and his family, had decided that the teen couple would get married. Susan was a junior in high school and three months pregnant. She and Randy had been dating for about a year. They were each other's first steady partner.

As the days turned into weeks and decisions about a wedding date and arrangements needed to be made, Susan seemed to hang back.

Her mother, Gail, grew suspicious of Susan's words, which said she wanted to get married, but might not reflect what she was really feeling inside.

Gail decided she would unravel what Susan's true feelings were, and her only real access to these was talk. She began to bring Susan into seemingly ordinary conversations about family-life topics. Examples from stories in the news, magazines, on television programs, and items of local happenings began to draw Susan out.

A news account of a runaway teen, for example, brought Susan to inappropriate anger. "That stupid girl!" she seethed. "How could she run away from her parents? Doesn't she know that's where she's safe?"

Viewing a talk show about women and self-esteem one day, Susan watched intently. A woman told her own story of having gotten into drug dealing and prostitution. The woman related that she had stopped such things and had developed self-esteem through the loving support of family and friends. Susan asked Gail, "How could she expect others to carry her load like that? How could they accept her after all she did?"

Adding up various pieces of information that Susan gave her unknowingly, Gail concluded that Susan really wanted to stay in the safety of their home, but felt so guilty and worthless about her pregnancy that she couldn't bring herself to tell them and ask for their help.

After careful thought, Gail confronted her daughter. Susan, flooded with emotional relief, confirmed Gail's suspicions and admitted she didn't really want to marry Randy at all, but she thought that she didn't deserve to ask any more of her parents than to help get her out of their home and on her own. She felt she had no choice.

By talking and listening, Gail was able to coax her daughter's true feelings out into the open. In the end, Gail convinced Susan she was not just a burden to her parents, and that they wanted her happiness above all else.

Susan and the others involved finally agreed that the

baby would be given up for adoption. Susan finished school, developed a career in a computer field, eventually married a different man, and now has three children within their happy family.

Talk! Talk! Talk! The choice is for a lifetime!

ABORTIONS

Libby, pregnant at 14, was rushed through an abortion at her parents' insistence. They did not consult with the boy who fathered the child or his parents. They simply sat Libby down, told her there was only one possible solution to her problem, and that they would make arrangements.

Libby knew, intellectually, what was going on, but she suppressed whatever feelings and questions she had because she felt she was at the total mercy of her parents.

The Nightmare Continues

Years later, however, Libby deeply regrets her inability to speak up then, and she resents her parents for their part in forcing the abortion on her.

At 30 and the mother of a much cherished five-year-old daughter, Libby says, "I still have a recurring nightmare about a faceless baby I am trying to rescue from several robed kidnappers. In it, I run and run. Just as the robed characters are to cross a point where I know I cannot rescue the baby, they turn, and each one has my face!"

Libby's haunting experience is not uncommon in adult women who had abortions as pregnant teens, especially those who later have other children. Often, they live with a shrouded guilt over the baby that they have allowed to be destroyed.

Lingering Resentments

Two years after her abortion, Shannon, 20, still gets tears in her eyes as she tells of her experience. "I hated myself for letting my parents talk me into it. I hated them for putting the importance of a college education over a child's life. I hated the baby's father for not wanting me to keep the baby!"

Shannon's reaction is also typical. Women who ride into an abortion on the tide of *getting rid of something that has inconvenienced the family* are often filled with turbulent hate and anger that must be worked through later.

Shannon continues. "An abortion is not a way to wrap the problem of a teen pregnancy into a neat little package! Life just isn't 'wrappable'! It may seem the easiest at the time but, in the end, it can be the hardest thing to deal with.

"I think I will always keep a wall between my parents and me over my abortion. It doesn't do much in the way of trusting others, either. My parents' judgment was more important to me than anyone else's. But when I needed them most, they abused my trust by forcing me to do what they wanted, not what I wanted!"

What God Has to Say

Jacquelyn talked to her pastor about her pregnancy. She asked him his opinion about abortions. He said, "Jacquelyn, you are 18 years old. You are not married and are too young to be a parent. However, that does not change the fact, that you are pregnant. I cannot advise that you have an abortion. There is a human being developing in your womb.

"The Holy Spirit enters a child upon its conception.

Luke 1:15 tells us: *He will be filled with the Holy Spirit even from birth.* When an abortion is performed it is a sin. It is killing a creation of God. Ecclesiastes 11:5 says: *As you do not know the path of the wind, or how the body is formed in a mother's womb, so you cannot understand the work of God, the Maker of all things.*

"And, probably the most dramatic statement of all is in Psalm 139:13-16. It leaves no question as to the presence of God in us from conception: *For you created my inmost being; you knit me together in my mother's womb. I praise you because I am fearfully and wonderfully made; your works are wonderful, I know that full well. My frame was not hidden from you when I was made in the secret place. When I was woven together in the depths of the earth, your eyes saw my unformed body. All the days ordained for me were written in your book before one of them came to be.*

"Jacquelyn, I would like to counsel you about other alternatives, in order to avoid your having an abortion."

The Importance of Counseling

Professional guidance, when a pregnant teen is considering having an abortion, is essential to her mental health, both for the near future and for several years later in her life.

Cindy, 28, did have an abortion when she was 16. "At the time, I wanted an abortion. My parents were completely against it. I went through with one anyway. There have been many repercussions. I was too young to understand the value of human life."

Cindy advises, "Anyone who is trying to determine if she will have an abortion should definitely do two things beforehand. One, get counseling. The issue of being a pregnant teen is emotional enough, but trying to handle the choice of abortion all alone at such a time is just too much. Second, if it is at all possible, talk to someone who has had an abortion. Listen to the real-life consequences from those who know.

"Fortunately, I had an excellent counselor who helped me work through the aftermath of my abortion. He helped guide me through my guilt. And, knowing God forgave me, I was able to forgive myself. I can now live with myself and know that I can't change what I let happen when I was too innocent to realize the magnitude of my actions. But the Lord has helped me to see how precious life is."

MARRIAGE

When Larry and Norma Johnson were told by 16-year-old Megan that she was pregnant, they were not terribly shocked. Like so many other parents, they had nervously observed their daughter's relationship with her boyfriend grow *too close for comfort.* They had lived in dread of her becoming pregnant many months before it actually happened.

In Spite of Doing the Right Things . . .

They did not want her to be pregnant. Larry and Norma had taken great pains to raise their three children conscientiously. A close family, Megan and her two brothers had enjoyed the privilege of parents who were fair, supportive, and loving.

The family attended church regularly and lived by Christian principles. Megan had grown up knowing that premarital sex was not morally right. She, as so many young women, had been overcome by the power of her changing body's sexual urges and her inner drive to connect with a loving mate. As many before her, once Megan was sexually involved, she thought there was no turning back.

Larry and Norma, sensing Megan's increasing closeness to her boyfriend, Thad, had been torn between what they feared was going on and what they deeply hoped wasn't. They had several conversations with Megan about abstinence. Megan repeatedly assured her parents that she understood what they were saying and that she realized the importance of what they told her.

Norma was realistic and open about the emotional waves that can overtake any two people in love. Megan seemed to sincerely absorb and digest the information. For all intents and purposes, Larry, Norma, and Megan had a family relationship where all the right things were done at the right time. A solid foundation had been laid for Megan's growing up.

However, Larry and Norma knew they could not force Megan into choices she did not want to make. They knew if they forbade her to see Thad, she might feel forced to sneak behind their backs and be driven deeper into his arms. So they lived between dread and hope.

For Megan, once she was sexually active, there seemed no rectifying the situation. She loved her parents very much and could not bear to disappoint them with any admissions about having sex with Thad. Therefore, she took the risk that she would not get pregnant, hoping that they need never know. Though the guilt of hiding such a thing from her parents weighed on her heavily, it was preferable to hurting them, and Megan justified the lie further by convincing herself that the love she had for Thad made it all right to keep their relationship private.

Facing the Situation

When Megan and Thad sat with Larry and Norma the first time after they knew Megan was expecting a child, there was a great tension in the room.

Norma looked at the two young people sitting side by side on the sofa with a mixture of sadness and concern. Larry was torn between anger at them both and some amount of thankfulness that at least the father of his grandchild was a decent boy.

Megan spoke first. "I know this isn't easy, but Thad and I have talked a lot about what to do, and we really want to get married."

Larry, Norma, and Megan had thoroughly discussed different options available to them with their pastor, then among themselves. Megan and Thad had talked together, and Larry and Norma had, also. Thad's parents had expressed their hope that the couple would get married, and offered their emotional and financial support toward this end.

Norma looked at her daughter and thought how very young she was. She said, "The important thing, kids, is that we stay objective. Marriage is an extremely tough prospect, and now is not the time to be noble."

"Yes," Larry added quickly, "you two are holding together very well under the circumstances. But you mustn't feel obliged to get married for anyone else's sake. There is no right or wrong thing to do here."

"Sir," Thad tentatively spoke, "I know what you and Mrs. Johnson are saying, and I respect your opinion. But I really love your daughter, and I want to marry her more than anything."

Inside, Larry caught himself wanting to laugh. Thad was as sincere as he could be, but there was an old-movie corniness to his words that belied his youthful age. The pastor had warned both Larry and Norma that many of the things the teenagers might say could sound very immature to the older, more experienced adults. However, he cautioned them to be considerate of what the youngsters said, and to remember that they were doing the best they could at their age. He said it was imperative that, in order to keep open communications, Larry and Norma bear in mind that the teens' feelings were genuine.

Norma interjected, "Thad, we do know that you love Megan, and she, you. But we are concerned that the two of you don't push for marriage because you feel you have no other choice.

"We realize that it's terribly frightening to discuss other choices, like adoption, and sometimes marriage seems the lesser of many evils. But the two of you have an entire lifetime ahead of you. Marriage is not the only way to handle this."

"Mom, we know that. Really, we do," Megan said. "But we have talked about marriage before, and the pregnancy has just pushed it ahead a few years."

"Then, Megan, you're saying you feel that you're making this choice freely?" Larry asked.

"Yes, Dad."

Larry turned toward the boy. "And you, Thad?"

"Yes, sir," Thad nodded.

"Well, then," Norma said, "I think for now the two of you need to talk to your parents, Thad. And Larry and I will discuss how we feel about your getting married, and our part in it."

Seeking Outside Help

Larry and Norma went back to the pastor with questions

regarding Megan and Thad getting married. Larry expressed a deep anxiety. "I feel such a responsibility! If we let them get married so young, knowing the odds against them making a marriage work are extremely high, it's as if we help set them up for a failure that could scar them for life."

"Larry, I understand your point," Pastor Greene responded. "But it is important that we examine some

You cannot make choices for them or pay their consequences.

facts here. Megan made the unfortunate choice to enter into a sexual relationship with Thad. She knows this is in direct conflict with her moral values. She also knows that with disobedience to any rule, whether that rule be yours at home, a law of the land, or one of God's, come certain consequences.

"Her consequence in this case is her pregnancy. Megan, like you or me, is a free agent. She must now make another important choice. Whatever that choice is will also bring its own set of consequences. If she chooses marriage to Thad, then rather than living in fear of their failure, you two might support and encourage them along the way to go the extra mile needed to make that marriage work."

No guarantees. "But," Larry said, "there aren't any guarantees."

"No," said Pastor Greene, "not from people—not for their marriage, yours, or mine. We live in trust that if we obey God's laws, our guarantee for success in whatever we do is inherent because we are Christians. Success may not be by our standards, but by God's. Obedience to Him, then, is the guarantee. If Megan and Thad's marriage doesn't work out down the road, then it is because they have not walked in obedience to God's laws and have freely chosen to act on their will. You cannot make choices for them or pay their consequences. You can only help to share the burdens and try to guide them on to make better choices in the future."

"But what is the potential of their marriage working, Pastor?" asked Norma.

"Well, with the sound relationship you two have with each other and with Megan, and considering that Thad is a sincere young man with his parents behind him, too, I'd say their chances are much better than most kids in their predicament. Often, my help is sought after all the pieces are broken. In this case, you have come before the situation got completely out of hand, and that is healthier by far."

How to help. "Okay," Norma said. "Then given that Megan sticks to wanting to get married, and that everyone is in agreement, how can we best help them?"

"I'd say, first, don't push them. Let Megan and Thad have the next several weeks to interact over the idea of getting married. There's no reason to rush. Hurrying a marriage will not make the pregnancy go away. And living at home for a while gives an excellent opportunity for you to observe how Megan's and Thad's personalities mesh. Do they strain to get along? Watch for basic problems in their relationship. Are their temperaments similar? Is one avidly seeking marriage and the other just going along, not really wanting to get married? Do they have similar interests, energy levels, etc.?

"Living with you also gives an opportunity to continue a sound nutritional and self-care environment for Megan. She needs proper rest and diet to support her body and the baby, more now than ever!"

Larry had another important subject in mind. "What about financial support, Pastor? How far should parents go in making it easy for these kids?"

Pastor Greene considered for several seconds before answering. "That is a tricky question, Larry. There is a fine line between encouraging self-support and just giving the kids hand-outs so they can live together under the pretense of marriage. This does no one any good. The couple needs to build up their self-esteem and prepare for a real marriage, not just playing house.

"If you can help guide Megan and Thad through realistic financial planning and establishing goals so they can see they will progress toward independence, then they will feel they are earning their right to take control of their future together as man and wife.

How not to help. "I recently counseled a family in which the parents were totally supporting the couple while the teens finished their last year of high school. Well-intentioned, to be sure, but this plan backfired miserably. The kids felt completely dependent on the parents (which, materially, they were), and they remained adolescent in their attitudes. The parents tried to exercise power over how the couple spent their money—complaining about social activities, eating-out habits, etc.—and the couple rebelled as if they were still teenagers at home. This did the teen couple's relationship great harm. They turned their frustrations toward each other and eventually split, largely because they had not developed a sense of needing one another, or paving their own way in life as a couple."

"But," Norma responded, "if Larry and I contribute to Megan and Thad's support, then I expect to have some say in how they live. For instance, we've considered turning our garage into a small cottage for them to live in. Are you saying we should tolerate noisy parties or their spending money foolishly at our expense?"

"No," Pastor Greene answered. "But perhaps here is one of the main problems I see in trying to overcome the difficulties in teen marriages. The couple is necessarily dependent on, most likely, his or her parents for help, and the parents may have a hard time not using that help to make the couple live the life-style the parents want. The couple resents this and feels vulnerable.

Laying the Ground Rules. "Much also depends on the parents' means and ability to help. In your case, with converting your garage, it is essential that guidelines and house rules be set up before the couple moves in. Like any other tenants, Megan and Thad should receive a written agreement about your policies. Are they going to pay rent? If so, how much and when? If they don't have cash, I would strongly urge a *work-to-earn* program so the couple feel they can pull their own weight each month. Maybe Megan could clean your home, and Thad could do yard work. Decide if they will have laundry privileges, a curfew, etc. Can they have pets? All these should be determined beforehand.

"In return—and this is a big one—you must respect their privacy, and they, yours. No walking in and out unannounced. No well-meant advice on their cleaning habits, etc. In other words, don't stand over them. They must learn on their own. And from the start, they should know you respect and sanction this requirement of any good relationship! They should know that if their budget calls for hamburger, then that's what they eat. No grabbing steaks from your refrigerator to make their life more comfortable. No taking advantage of watching your color television because they don't like their black-and-white. Certainly, there are exceptions but, basically, you do Megan and Thad no favors by letting them wear rose-colored glasses. You do yourselves no favors by encouraging them to be dependent on you.

"Don't strain your finances to the limit, either. You will only resent them for it. Better for them that they live in a small apartment and eat at a cardboard table on their own than feel responsible for your financial demise. If they must quit school for now to earn their living, well, then, it costs money to live, and they should know that right off."

"But the harder they have it," Larry said, "the more chance they won't make it together. Then, feasibly, we could end up with Megan and a baby at our door."

"I don't completely agree with that, Larry," Pastor Greene answered. "People are often more resilient than we give them credit for. James 1:2-4 tells us: *Consider it pure joy, my brothers, whenever you face trials of many kinds, because you know that the testing of your faith develops perseverance. Perseverance must finish its work so that you may be mature and complete, not lacking anything.*

"So it seems best not to make things too easy on them. If you and Norma help them financially, then do so within a comfortable limit for you; outline exactly what you expect from them in return for this help and, thereafter, mind your own business."

Helping them prepare. "Pastor," Norma asked, "I still don't understand how we can prepare them for the struggles of marriage. Are there guidelines you can give us?"

"Yes," Pastor Greene said, "the first is to tell them to

discuss their individual needs, fears, feelings, and hopes with each other. Communication is probably the single most important ingredient in a healthy relationship. Others cannot know how we feel unless we tell them.

"Second, advise them that when particular problems keep coming up, they must do whatever has to be done to settle them. Whether that means getting professional help or not, the key is that recurring problems always require compromise. Both partners must give something to make the issue resolvable for them as a couple.

"Third, emphasize that relationships do have problems. By accepting this and letting time pass during a crisis, troubles are often kept in perspective. Problems don't seem nearly so overwhelming if one or both partners can say, 'Hey, everybody goes through this. Let's be calm for tonight and see how we feel in the morning.' I call this positive procrastination.

"Fourth, tell them to relax and enjoy the present. Life can be harsh, but the more one can master living each day as it comes, the more easily one enjoys everyday things.

"Matthew 6:34 says: *Therefore do not worry about tomorrow, for tomorrow will worry about itself. Each day has enough trouble of its own.* Megan and Thad should be encouraged to be thankful for each day's blessings and trials.

"Lastly, but most importantly, tell Megan and Thad, and I will, also, that no matter what life brings them, Jesus waits, in good times and in bad, to commune with them in their life. Nothing scares Him away—He will not reject them! Hebrews 4:15 and 16 says: *For we do not have a high priest who is unable to sympathize with our weaknesses, but we have one who has been tempted in every way, just as we are—yet was without sin. Let us then approach the throne of grace with confidence, so that we may receive mercy and find grace to help us in our time of need."*

As Norma and Larry finished this consultation, they felt much more confident that they could help Megan and Thad if marriage was indeed their choice. Pastor Greene was an immense help to the family in their search for answers.

SINGLE PARENTING

Deb Easton, 15, was frantic when she found out she was pregnant. She begged her doctor to give her an abortion. There was no calming her. The doctor called Deb's parents at their respective places of work to come to his office.

Jack and Louise Easton were totally shocked at the news of Deb's pregnancy. She had been dating Peter less than six months! They had only met the boy a few times as the two left the house on dates.

Considering Deb's panic and the circumstances, the doctor immediately recommended a psychologist for the family to consult.

In counseling, it came to light that Deb had fallen into a sexual relationship with Peter after a party where she had consumed enough alcohol to eliminate any inhibitions she might otherwise have had. Not having the self-esteem to turn Peter's advances away on other occasions, Deb had never dreamed she would get pregnant. She barely knew the mechanics of sex, and thought she would have to have her period for several years before her body would accommodate a baby.

It was also obvious that Jack and Louise were very uncomfortable with the subject of sex, and had referred to it in their home as something only adults needed to know about. It was kept a very private, guarded topic, and Deb had harbored a deep fear of exposing her sexual activity. Just the thought of telling her parents about her pregnancy had made an abortion sound preferable.

Dealing with the Father's Family

It was quickly established, however, that an abortion was out of the question. Thereafter, marriage was also ruled out. Like Deb, Peter was only 15. The teens were both freshmen in high school, and hardly knew each other. Peter's parents were adamant that they wanted nothing to do with a baby; they would pay for an abortion or any adoptive procedures, but that was as far as they would be involved. The psychologist informed the Easton family that, should Deb keep her baby, Peter and his family might very well have a legal obligation to help support the child financially. He advised them that they should contact an attorney on that matter.

He also advised them to think this over very carefully, noting that to force a relationship with a reluctant father was a tricky situation, especially when they hardly knew him. The psychologist pointed out that the lifetime commitment of parenting was complex at best, and to throw in additional complications for the sake of money alone did not necessarily warrant the tensions and heartache that might come with it.

On the other hand, if Peter insisted that, as the baby's father, he would take some responsibility and did want a relationship with his child, then he had that right; with this could come another unique set of problems. For now, though, it appeared that the main priority was to decide what to do; the burden of this decision rested with the Eastons.

Agreeing on a Course of Action

Jack Easton, watching his oldest daughter across the breakfast table one morning did not think he could bear to see her give up her child for adoption, which was one of only two options they were considering. The other was single parenting. Jack felt that he and Louise should see Deb all the way through her pregnancy, keep her at home, and help her raise the baby.

Louise, on the other hand, was quite confused about this direction. They had Deb and her two younger brothers, Mark, twelve, and Jason, nine, at home. Louise was concerned about the precedent Deb's pregnancy might set for the boys, and the adverse effects a new baby in their home might have on all of them. Sibling rivalry and jealousy among brothers and sisters was one thing, but to have this magnified in a grandchild/nephew or niece was in the forefront of Louise's mind.

In addition to all that, she didn't know that she could handle another child emotionally. At 39, Louise had hoped her middle years would be more carefree, having previously put aside some of her own personal goals for when her children were older. She was looking forward to pursuing hobbies, redecorating the house, and maybe even putting in a swimming pool.

In counseling, Louise expressed her resentment of Jack's assuming that *of course* it would be fine for Deb to keep the baby and live at home. For Louise, this represented a confinement of her own time and resources. A confrontation was inevitable.

"It's easy for you to say, Jack!" Louise blurted out one day. "You go to work every day. I'm the one who will be at home with a baby! I'm the one who will be tied down, doing the cooking, the cleaning, and the chasing!"

"I didn't say Deb's life would continue as usual," Jack argued. "I figured she'd have to have a sitter and help carry the load. I don't mean you should take on her baby as if it were your own."

Louise was not at all consoled. "Be realistic! Where is Deb going to get the money for day care, diapers, formula, clothes, etc.? From our pocket! That's a drain on our money, and means sacrifices for everyone, including the boy's. Is that fair to them?"

Jack did not hesitate. "Louise, we are a family! We need to look out for our own. If it means some changes, well, then, we'll have to make the best of them. We can't desert Deb now when she needs us, and we can't give our grandchild away!"

What Does the Teen Want?

The psychologist interrupted. "Jack, Louise, it is not going to help matters for your relationship to sustain irreparable damage over Deb's pregnancy. I think we need to back up and ask some pertinent questions and search for answers that you can all live with, including Deb!

"It is also important to remember that you are in a position to guide Deb, not tell her what to do. This is a most delicate situation. Trying to force her into keeping a baby she really doesn't want, or giving one up that she does want, can carve deep wounds into all of you."

Jack and Louise agreed that they had gotten ahead of themselves and should start over with the two options the family would consider. They started with Deb's feelings. She was firm that she wanted to keep the baby. But she had also overheard some of her parents' arguments about this, and was concerned over the effects on them.

The psychologist asked Deb, "If you could have things

totally how you wanted, how would they be?"

Deb answered, "I've thought about it a lot, and at first I wanted the baby and me to be by ourselves in an apartment or something. But then I knew that wouldn't be the best for me or the baby. I don't know a lot of the stuff I need to know about being a mother or running a house.

"So, I guess, mostly, I would want to be close to Mom and Dad, but still be on my own. I want to finish school, but I don't want Mom to have to baby-sit, so I guess I'd have to get a job. I don't want to hurt Mark and Jason, and I know it's selfish to think I can just live at home, but I'm willing to help there, too."

Talking It Through

The psychologist then asked, "Deb, do you understand that a baby takes a tremendous amount of time and energy?"

"Kind of," Deb said. "I know I can't understand it all. But I remember a little about when Jason was born. Mom was tired a lot, and moody. And she didn't have as much time for Mark and me. But I'll only have one baby to watch out for."

Louise was amazed at Deb's sensitivity in the discussion. She had anticipated totally childish expectations. Jack's heart warmed as he saw his daughter rising to the occasion of problem-solving and his wife relaxing a little.

The psychologist addressed Louise. "Can you tell us something about when you were a new mother and Deb was your only baby?"

"Well," Louise began, "I was very frightened at home alone with her. I wasn't sure I'd know what to do with a baby. Jack's mom came to stay the second and third weeks after Deb was born. By that time, being a new mother seemed *old hat,* and I was glad to see her go."

Louise laughed at the memory of herself as a young mother. "But when she'd been gone another two weeks, I wished like anything she'd come back! Deb was up at nights crying with colic. We were exhausted. Jack couldn't help every night because he needed rest to be able to work. I napped off and on during the day, so the laundry and housework piled up. I prayed a lot!

"Then, when she was about three months old, things settled down a bit. We got into a routine and enjoyed her more. I felt better, more confident. The next hard time came when she could get around. She crawled all over and couldn't be trusted a minute by herself!"

Louise ran a hand down Deb's long brown hair and smiled at her fondly. "But I wouldn't take back a day of it! She was the most precious, wonderful baby!" Tears from a mother's full heart escaped onto Louise's cheeks, and Deb put her arms around her mother's neck. Jack wiped at his own tears as the two most important women in his life wept with love for each other. The release was a turning point for the Easton family.

Implementing the Decision

They eventually decided that Deb would keep her baby. After discussing apartments and remodeling their own home, they decided that, since they lived in an area with enough space, they would put a small mobile home on their property for Deb and the baby to live in. This would provide breathing room for every member of the family, and interfere the least with their life-style. Louise could still redecorate and pursue her hobbies, but conceded that a swimming pool wasn't nearly as important as a grandchild. Mark and Jason could benefit from learning to share their lives with a baby, but still not sacrifice their relationship with their parents.

In return for her parents buying the mobile home, Deb would clean their house and do odd jobs once a week. The family was introduced to a high school completion program for pregnant teens by the school guidance counselor.

The teen has to realize that her actions have changed the whole family's life, and she must give her share to minimize these changes, while still keeping her dignity intact.

Through it, Deb would attend classes in the mornings, with day care provided. She would be placed in a career-oriented, apprenticeship-type job in the afternoons. This program was available until enough high school credits had been earned for Deb to graduate.

Louise agreed that she would care for the baby in the afternoons while Deb worked, and one evening a week while she spent time alone or socialized. Jack agreed that he would take Louise out for a special time together one evening a week, and Deb would keep an eye on Mark and Jason.

The money Deb earned in the weekday afternoons was only enough for the extreme basics of survival. Since Jack and Louise could comfortably help, they agreed that, if Deb would do things like errands and grocery shopping, they would supplement her income on a weekly basis.

This arrangement was carefully outlined and agreed on by all the Eastons, including Mark and Jason.

A Livable Plan for Everyone

Since single parenting is the most involved for families of pregnant teens, it is imperative that each member of the family have a say, and all affected agree on a plan. The teen has to realize that her actions have changed the whole family's life, and she must give her share to minimize these changes, while still keeping her dignity intact.

With this choice, like any other, there is no going back. It should not be made hastily, or with a basis in pride. The world will go on and time will heal many wounds if an option is undertaken in an open, loving spirit.

In preparing for this situation, it is also absolutely necessary to have ground rules, not only for the living arrangements and the teen's interaction with the family, but also for the relationships each person will have with the baby. The teen is the mother, and she needs to be respected as such. It can be a large temptation for the grandparents to take over their daughter's attempts to parent in her own way. Unless there is something that is urgently endangering the child or teen's well-being, it is best not to give advice unless asked. The teen has the right to make her own mistakes, just like any other parent.

Likewise, however, the teen should not be allowed to manipulate her family because of her circumstances. There is bound to be a certain adolescent attitude in the way she approaches things; a pregnant teen does not automatically become an adult. If she uses her condition inappropriately, this should promptly be taken up with a professional's help.

Deb went through a period where she wasn't holding up her end of the agreement for doing chores around the Eastons' home. When Jack and Louise confronted her, she threw a childish tantrum about being too tired to do laundry, and if they didn't like it she just wouldn't visit them when the baby was born. As this was obviously unacceptable behavior, the family, after attempts to work it out at home failed, went back to the psychologist's office. There they worked through the problems together.

There are circumstances where more intense care for the teen is needed. If she has severe morning sickness, for example, or other restrictive health factors, she may require bedrest or other precautionary treatment. If, for instance, she has to have a caesarean delivery, she will need to be helped a great deal more after the child's birth. Discuss your teen's needs with her medical doctor.

Further, not all families have the financial means to help as much as the Eastons did. Many families must worry about keeping food on the table, rather than giving up a swimming pool, and these are real considerations that need real exploration. There may be financial and/or healthcare aid available in your area. Contact your city, county and/or state Social Services Agency. Someone there will be able to help you with information about the issues that concern you.

ADOPTION

Deciding to give up a child may be the hardest choice of all for a pregnant teen and her family. Quite often, it is the most emotionally charged choice, as well. It requires much prayer, soul-searching, and cooperation. In Matthew 7:7,8, Jesus tells us: *Ask and it will be given to you; seek and you will find; knock and the door will be opened to you. For everyone who asks receives; he who seeks finds; and to him who knocks, the door will be opened.*

A Lifetime Decision

Because everyone involved lives with the adoption for the rest of their lives, it is important not to try to push this option on a young girl. Carla, 26, says, "I have a baby girl in the world, somewhere, who doesn't know me. She doesn't know that my parents coerced me into giving her away over 10 years ago! Sometimes, I still resent them for it. And there's nothing I can do to make amends. Even if I spent the next several years in an all-out search for her, found her, and explained everything to her, what good would it do? Oh, my conscience might be clear temporarily, but I would throw her, her parents, and myself into total turmoil!

"If my parents had been a little more patient, I probably would have come to the decision myself. I needed counseling, but they were too ashamed to get it for me. Consequently, I am left with a permanent, wondering void in my life.

"I know my parents live with it, and have suffered greatly, too. But it still doesn't erase my pain."

Carla's sister, Joanie, at 29 and with two children of her own, has also experienced lasting effects due to her sister's trauma. "If only Mom and Dad had been more understanding of Carla's dilemma! I tried to talk them into seeking professional help, but they wouldn't listen. I've always felt guilty, like I should have been able to do something to stop them!

"I don't know if Carla will ever have other children after the heartbreak she went through. My parents practically locked her in her room the whole time she was pregnant. They wouldn't let the baby's father visit or even talk to her on the phone! She had to stay back a grade in school for all the time she missed. I was only 19 myself, so, even though I sympathized, my own social life seemed more important at the time. I feel guilty for having had the youth Carla lost. I even feel guilty about having two healthy kids!"

Carla's parents, Gwen and Chuck, have also agonized over the way they handled her pregnancy. They still cannot discuss it openly. Gwen will only say, "We made a terrible mistake with Carla, but it was the best we knew how to do at the time."

Carla remembers the pregnancy as clearly as though it were yesterday. "It was bad enough, having to be in the same house with them, but to grow bigger and bigger with the baby kicking inside of me, and my parents looking at me with disgust, that was horrible torture! If my parents ever doubted their decision, they never showed it to me."

Not the Easy Way Out

On the other hand, 13-year-old Stacy's parents did express doubts over the family decision to give her baby up for adoption. Clare Houston says now, nearly 20 years later, that she and her husband, John, still wince over the tearing apart they felt long ago.

"Oh, how we went around and around! Stacy was so young. In the beginning, she was more concerned with the restrictions on her social activities than the baby. She is a very loving, good parent to the two children she has now; but, at 13, a girl cannot know her heart or mind.

"She was agreeable enough to an adoption, but John and I had doubts. As the baby grew and Stacy could feel life, she began to doubt, too. Poor thing, it was as if she grew up overnight! Adopting out a child is not the easy way out. Families should know that it takes a huge amount of love and courage on everyone's part to get through it.

"When Stacy delivered a perfect baby boy, she was like a trembling animal trapped in a corner. She was devastated. As long as I live, I will not forget the grief of seeing that tiny infant through the nursery window one day, and an empty bassinet the next. John and I felt like criminals.

"Even though the baby was gone to a new life, to us it felt like he was dead. There was a hollowness to our lives for months afterward. For all practical purposes, it was the grieving process of death that our family went through. Had we not had our Christian faith, I don't know how we could have gotten through it.

"During that time, a dear friend sent me a card with Psalm 34:18 written on it. It said: *The Lord is close to the brokenhearted and saves those who are crushed in spirit.* I saved that card, and it has more teardrops on it than I care to recall."

Finding an Inner Strength

Stephanie, at 18, faced the decision of giving her baby up pretty much on her own. Her father, a hopeless alcoholic, was not one bit sympathetic. In his worst moments, he called her a slut and, at his best, he called her stupid. Stephanie's mother was so afraid of her husband that she nearly pleaded with Stephanie to get an abortion in order to make life easier on the household. But Stephanie was not to be pushed. She arranged to live with her grandmother, went to counseling, and, with her head held high, gave her baby up for adoption.

Today, six years later, she still feels she made the best choice. "My pregnancy was a huge shock that woke me up to a lot of things. Through it, I realized that it was the result of a desperate search on my part to find a man to love and approve of me like my father never had.

"When he found out I was pregnant, my boyfriend dumped me. I was almost crazy with fear. But a friend of mine, whose family had always been kind to me and knew about my home life, took me to see her pastor. He talked to me about Jesus and the salvation available through Him. He spoke of all the wonderful things that Christians are privileged to have in their lives with Christ. He assured me that Christians have sorrows, too, but that, through Jesus, all things are possible.

"I gave my problems over to Him, like it says in Matthew 11:28 to 30: *Come to me, all you who are weary and burdened, and I will give you rest. Take my yoke upon you and learn from me, for I am gentle and humble in heart, and you will find rest for your souls. For my yoke is easy and my burden is light.*

"The inner strength I needed to make my decisions, to live through my pregnancy, to give up my child, and to get my life back in order came from the wellspring of Jesus' power. My child is better off—I know it—with parents who love her and can raise her to be a whole adult. It wasn't easy, but it was right."

Giving a child to someone who is better able to provide a stable home life is one of the most difficult, complex decisions a family ever has to make. There are no clear-cut rights or wrongs, no definite lines with which to measure one's motives, failure or success. The single thing everyone agrees on is that it is painful.

One important aspect of carrying through on an adoption is the agency and/or attorney involved. There are many ways to go about an adoption these days, and each offers its own set of advantages and complications. Families seeking help in this area should contact their family physician, attorney and/or Social Service Agency.

Teri's Story

Teri Wilson, 19, was referred to an attorney by her doctor. She spoke to him alone at first. Scott, the attorney, asked Teri many questions about her pregnancy, including, "Teri, how do you feel toward the baby's father? Is there any chance of you two getting together?"

Teri replied quickly. "Oh, no! The way it happened is hard to tell you. But the baby's father is actually a married man, almost 20 years older than I am."

Blushing, Teri paused in order to gauge the attorney's reaction. Her parents had been hysterical when she told them about her affair. She didn't want to go through a scene with the attorney, too.

Scott, noting Teri's expression, opened a door for trusting communication. "You know, Teri, this is not at all uncommon. These things do happen. And you are very brave to consider handling your pregnancy through an adoption."

Teri sighed audibly. "Well, I'm glad you aren't going to pass judgment on me, like my parents did. I thought Dad was going to have a stroke! They don't realize how rotten this all is for me. I didn't know the guy was married until a few weeks before I found out I was pregnant. He had told me he was out-of-town a lot on business. I believed him until I saw him in a restaurant with his wife.

"At first, he tried to convince me he really loved me. But when he found out I was expecting his baby, he was quick to stop any pretending. He tried to cover up any responsibility for the baby by ranting and raving that I was probably sleeping around and maybe he wasn't the father, which is untrue on both counts."

Teri felt a lump rise in her throat and had to pause, but Scott smoothly picked up the conversation while she regained her composure. "I'm sure this is awfully hard for you, Teri, and I truly do sympathize with you. I wish I didn't even have to ask you about the baby's father, but it is important to determine the likelihood of the biological parents getting together and deciding to keep the baby."

"No," Teri shook her head, "I am positive an adoption is best for all concerned, especially the baby. Considering that I'm in college now, what my family's reaction is, that I would have to find a way to support us, and the situation with the father, I'm afraid I would resent the child and not be a good parent."

"There are counseling programs, Teri," Scott said, "if you feel that professional guidance would help you keep your baby."

"No." Teri was firm. "What is this? Don't you want me to give up the baby?"

"I don't believe that's for me to say," Scott was cautious not to scare Teri away. "It is my job, however, to make sure that I aid you in doing the best thing possible for you, the baby, and the adoptive parents. That means I have to ask some pretty painful questions at times. If you really did want to keep your baby and were here only because you felt you had nowhere else to turn, I would get you to the help you needed; that's all."

Searching for the right parents. Teri's guard came down once again; Scott was not out to hurt her. "Okay. Thanks, but I know inside that adoption is the best. Don't get me wrong, I'd do anything if I could erase all this, or if the baby's father and I were in love and could get married, but . . . " Teri paused to collect her emotions.

"It's all right, Teri," Scott said. "Let's talk about a different part of this for now. What I have for you, as the biological mother, is a portfolio of what I'll call résumés.

These are from qualified couples and individuals who are prospective parents. Together, we will determine what you hope for in the way of parents and a home for the baby you're carrying. I'll then be able to narrow the number of résumés to about 8 or 10 for your review. We'll cut that down again to a few adoptive parents who specifically fit your preferences. You will then receive packets of more in-depth information, provided by them, about their lives, their pasts, the present, and goals for the future. Maybe one or two couples will be eliminated right away because of something that is in direct conflict with your beliefs or desires. Follow me so far?"

Teri nodded. "Yes. I feel really nervous but, in a small way, it's like an adventure."

"That is a good attitude, Teri," Scott responded. "You are in a position, as nearly as is humanly possible, to insure your child's well-being. What you're doing is one of the most courageous, compassionate things any parent can do for a child, as well as for the adoptive parents. I admire you deeply for this!"

Teri looked Scott in the eyes. "I don't know if it's like you say, or whether I'm just selfish. Only time will tell, but thanks for your vote of confidence."

Scott also spoke to Teri's parents, Lorna and Bruce Wilson, who seemed cold and unapproving. He explained the process of choosing possible adoptive parents to them. Bruce was mortified. "Sounds like shopping for used cars to me! Why, you're making this sound like a reward for Teri's having gotten herself into this mess, instead of paying for her mistake!"

"Mr. Wilson," Scott bristled, "it is not for me to punish Teri. Teri is punishing herself enough. I am here in order to make an extremely difficult situation as easy as possible. If there are moments of hope and optimism, then so much the better, but I assure you it is much more complex than shopping for an automobile!"

Bruce Wilson was skeptical. "Well, I don't like it."

Scott was anxious to get the meeting over with, and Lorna and Bruce left a short time later.

Together, Scott and Teri chose two couples who Teri felt would provide excellent homes for the baby she carried. Scott then had Teri carefully give him her own background, personal information, and feelings about the pregnancy. His secretary typed it into a résumé, similar to that of the prospective parents, and Teri wrote a cover letter to each of the hopeful couples. Scott sent these packets to each of the two couples chosen, and received replies within a week.

Face-to-face meetings. Both couples, living in different areas away from the region where Teri lived, agreed to a meeting with Teri at Scott's office on separate days.

The first couple was warm and open. They let Teri ask all the questions from a list she had prepared, and answered them without hesitation. Teri felt good about this couple immediately. They took her out to lunch. There was a rapport, which Scott sensed would culminate in an adoption, but he insisted Teri should meet the other couple in order to have a definite comparison.

It was to be a real contrast. The second couple was much more reserved in their approach to Teri. They were similar in background and financial means to the first couple, but Teri just didn't feel as certain of them.

Later, Teri expressed that she did not want to hurt the second couple. "They were nice," she told Scott, "but I know the first couple are the ones for this baby. I don't want the second couple to feel like they weren't good enough, though."

"That's one of the down-side risks on the adoptive parents' side of the fence, Teri," Scott said. "It's sad, but they know going in that this is one of the things they will face, maybe several times, before they find the right match in an expectant mother.

"I have counseled with each couple in my files, and they are as prepared as can be expected not to take things like this as a personal rejection. When I tell them of your decision, I am as gentle as I can be, and as optimistic of the future as possible."

Getting acquainted. In the weeks following, Teri received more written information directly from the first couple, telling her about themselves, their respective families, and their feelings about meeting Teri.

The three met in Scott's office again about a month later. There were a few strained moments when the adoptive parents noted Teri's stomach, which, by now, was obviously protruding. Also, Teri had been feeling life from within, and the situation was becoming more real to everyone involved. Scott, having seen this stage of things many times, dealt with it directly.

The couple said that they were afraid to get too excited about Teri's baby, in case she backed out.

"Then, we would be devastated," said Jake.

Teri assured them they had nothing to worry about, but Scott cautioned her. "Teri, Bonnie and Jake know that you mean well and are sincere. But another risk adoptive parents live with is that you will change your mind. You know that, legally, in this state, you actually have up to 90 days after the baby's birth in which to change your mind. That is sensible protection for you. Bonnie and Jake know they must live with this. The three of you need to take things one day at a time."

Over the next four months, Teri talked with Bonnie and Jake on the phone every couple of weeks. They wrote letters back and forth and met twice more. It was agreed that Bonnie and Jake would save photos, a letter to the baby, and a few pieces of memorabilia, provided by Teri, for later on when the child would inevitably want to know about his or her mother. It was also agreed that Teri would see the child once in the 90-day period following the baby's birth, at Bonnie and Jake's home, to make sure she could go through with the adoption.

During this time, Teri also had the distasteful task of approaching the biological father to get his signature of release for the adoption. He signed immediately, saying only, "Smart kid!" When he walked away without another word, Teri wondered if she would ever trust anyone again.

Living arrangements. Teri's mother, Lorna, became more pleasant toward Teri as the time neared for the baby's delivery. Lorna was torn between empathy for her daughter and not wanting to prompt abrasive outbursts from her husband. Bruce Wilson refused to give one bit to the situation, and barely spoke to Teri at all during the long months. As soon as Teri had the baby, she would move to the nearby college dorms to give the broken relationship with her father time to start mending.

Had Teri been unable to tolerate the environment in her parents' home, or had they forced her out, Bonnie and Jake were prepared to pay for her living expenses. Teri felt it best to try and stick it out at home.

Financially, Bonnie and Jake were paying for all the prenatal care expenses, as well as those related to the baby's birth, adoption, and any unexpected costs. They had also offered Teri a $5,000 Savings Bond voluntarily, but Teri had refused their generosity. She told them that later she would feel as though she had sold her baby, rather than given it up.

The birth. The morning that Teri first experienced labor pains, she called Bonnie and Jake immediately. Bonnie was silent for several seconds on the other end of the line, 300 miles north of where Teri lived.

"Well," Teri went on, "this is it, I guess."

Bonnie began to cry. "Oh, Teri, I'm sorry," she said brokenly. "I'm just so nervous—and afraid."

"Don't be afraid," Teri said stoically. "I won't back out."

"No!" Bonnie cried. "That's not my fear. I'm afraid for you, for the baby, and for us! Teri, we've really grown fond of you, and we do wish you well."

"Thank you, Bonnie." It was Teri's turn to choke up. "Well, I'll see you guys when you get to the hospital."

As Teri hung up the phone, she turned to see her father, his face ghostly white, in the doorway. "I'm going to have the baby, Dad," she said. "You and Mom can be at the hospital, too, if you want."

"Girl," Bruce Wilson said, shaking his head, "I have to give you credit—you've got guts! I don't know that I can stand being there, but your mother will go. But I have to tell you, I think you're making a big mistake."

"I know, Dad," Teri said sadly. "I hope someday you'll understand."

Later that evening, Teri delivered a healthy baby girl. Bonnie and Jake named her Josalyn. Teri held her once before a nurse took her to a special room where she was united with her new parents. Teri lay there, seriously doubting her decision for the first time. The baby was perfect, soft and pink, with lots of brown hair. She had instinctively grasped at Teri's finger. When the nurse took Josalyn from her, Teri felt as if a part of her were dying.

Feeling very alone and empty, Teri was grateful to see her mother come to the room. Lorna hugged her daughter, and they wept together.

Going home. Bonnie and Jake came to Teri's room the next afternoon just as the young woman finished dressing to go home and recuperate. There was a bouquet of roses from Scott on her nightstand, and Bonnie went to admire them. She turned, standing close to Teri, then reached spontaneously to gather the girl in her arms. "Oh, Teri," Bonnie sobbed, "how can you ever know the precious gift you've given us, or how much love we have in our hearts for you and Josalyn?"

Teri returned the hug. "Bonnie, I think I'm only beginning to realize that; and, even though I'm hurting, I'm glad it's you and Jake who will raise her."

"Who's going to get you home?" Jake asked gently.

Teri wiped at her eyes. "My mom."

Jake put a hand on her shoulder. "Why don't you come to the nursery with us to say good-bye to Josalyn until you come to see her at our house?"

The three walked to the nursery, and Teri stood between Josalyn's parents, as they all watched the sleeping girl.

It was time to go. Teri knew it. She looked up and, in the hallway on the other side of the plate glass window, stood her father. With hands clasped in front of him, tears streamed down his leathered face.

Saying good-bye. Two months later, Teri visited Bonnie, Jake, and Josalyn. Their home was warm and open, just as Teri had expected. Scott and Teri's mother were with her. They all exchanged polite conversation and exclamations over Josalyn's beauty. Bonnie and Jake seemed to be holding their breath. Finally, Teri said, "I won't take her from you. She belongs here with you!"

Painful choices often carry painful consequences. Giving up a baby is the epitome of this pain. It can also be one of the deepest expressions of true love some young women can make in this world.

Lorna put a protective arm around her daughter. "It's all right, Teri. Everything will be fine."

The visit lasted only minutes longer. Lorna held Josalyn once. Teri kissed the child good-bye on the top of her head. Then they were gone.

Teri got through her ordeal by depending on her Christian faith. She handled it with a maturity beyond her years, in the face of her father's disapproval and her mother's less than full support. Teri had written a Scripture onto a scrap of paper when she first decided to give her baby up for adoption. Over the many months, it had become worn and tear-stained, but had given Teri the strength to follow her heart. John 15:13 says: *Greater love has no one than this, that he lay down his life for his friends.* In her agony, Teri had laid down her own life, that Josalyn might have a chance to live a happy, full one.

Painful choices often carry painful consequences. Giving up a baby is the epitome of this pain. It can also be one of the deepest expressions of true love some young women can make in this world. In John 15:12, Jesus says: *My command is this: Love each other as I have loved you.* Obedience to this command can be very difficult but, ultimately, fulfilling.

Teri Wilson finished college, married a wonderful man who loves her very much and, together, they have four sons. Teri teaches in a public school system in a metropolitan area.

LIVING AWAY FROM HOME

When Denise, 15, got pregnant, her parents, Sam and Lillian Costa, were so hostile toward her that there was no talking to them. She struggled through several days of cold silence before going to the school guidance counselor. Desperately, Denise begged for help. The counselor promised to do what she could. She phoned Denise's parents only to be told to mind her own business. She asked the principal to try to get Denise's parents to the school for a conference. They wouldn't come. Meanwhile, Denise was so miserable that she couldn't stand being at home. One morning, she filled her backpack with clothes instead of books, then left a note on her bed that said she wasn't coming home but would call to let them know she was okay.

This finally broke through her parents' icy silence. When Denise called that evening to say she was staying at a girlfriend's, her mother was frantic. "Denise!" she cried, "you must come home!"

Denise refused, and said she would only meet her parents in the presence of the counselor at school the next day. After several minutes of arguing, Denise's mother agreed.

A Professional Mediator

The next afternoon, Denise walked shakily into the counselor's office. Her parents were already there. They didn't speak to Denise, merely nodding at her as she sat down.

The room was tensely quiet for several seconds before Lillian Costa spoke sharply, glaring at the counselor, Miss Shaw. "Well, let's get on with this. I don't understand what you've got to do with our family business!"

Miss Shaw raised her eyebrows. "Mrs. Costa, I have no desire to interfere with your private lives. But Denise came to me for help. As a counselor for her school, it is my job and my wish to help her."

"Ha!" Sam Costa responded. "Too bad she didn't come to you before she got herself pregnant!"

"Mr. Costa," Miss Shaw answered, "I am not here to argue with you, and rudeness will get us nowhere. The fact is that Denise did get pregnant, and now she needs our help."

Sam Costa scowled at Miss Shaw, then looked disgustedly at his daughter. "See what you've gotten us into? Now, I not only have a pregnant kid, but I'm subjected to this woman's impertinence!"

After almost an hour of going back and forth with the Costas in this manner, Miss Shaw was totally frustrated. They were obviously not going to bend at all.

Denise had been a change-of-life baby for the couple, who were previously childless for nearly 30 years. They were humiliated beyond endurance by Denise's pregnancy. Miss Shaw could see it was useless. There was absolutely no getting along with the girl's parents.

"Perhaps the best thing would be for Denise to spend her pregnancy at a home where there are other teenage girls who are also pregnant."

"A home for unwed mothers, you mean?" Lillian Costa said with contempt.

"Fine by us," Sam added.

Miss Shaw tried to coax them into a more sympathetic line of thinking. "What I mean is, in this type of environment, Denise needn't feel so alone, and she can get professional guidance in deciding what to do about the baby.

Residential care programs are not just for teens in Denise's dire emotional circumstances. However, the sheer number of pregnant teens, complicated by lack of funds and space, often necessitates that those in greatest need are given first consideration.

You two could probably visit her and attend counseling sessions. Maybe that would help you understand why Denise got pregnant."

"We already know why she got pregnant, young woman, and don't you be sarcastic with us!" Sam exploded.

Miss Shaw could hardly contain her impatience. "I was not trying to be sarcastic. I was referring to the reasons behind Denise's sexual relationship, Mr. Costa." Miss Shaw wondered privately how anyone in this day and age could be so archaic in their reaction to such a common problem.

"Well," Lillian Costa broke in, "we don't need any counseling. But it would be just fine with us if Denise stayed in one of those homes. We love our daughter, Miss Shaw, and we'll take her back home after she gives the baby away."

Miss Shaw bit her bottom lip. "I see," she said. "Well, let me check with the local Family Planning Clinic and see if they can recommend a good program for Denise. I will find out the particulars, including costs."

"I'll pay it," Sam Costa said, as if he were a patron contributor to a worthwhile but distasteful cause. "Like the wife said, we love our daughter."

"I'd like Denise to stay awhile longer to talk with me, please," Miss Shaw said, as Sam rose from his chair.

"That's fine," Sam turned at the door and looked back at Denise. "But you best be home tonight, daughter, or else!"

With that, the parents left. Miss Shaw looked at the poor, dejected teen sitting on a chair near her. This child urgently needed professional help. Miss Shaw talked to Denise with gentle support.

Within two weeks, Denise was placed into a residential program for pregnant teens. Intense therapy during her pregnancy prepared Denise for eventually giving up the baby she delivered five months later. Periodic counseling sessions thereafter got her through the next two years at home with her parents. Although the Costas never broke stride in their cold, unyielding attitude, they loved Denise in the only way they knew how.

Sadly, even with counseling, Denise got pregnant again just after her eighteenth birthday. Sam and Lillian Costa sent their daughter packing. She married the boy who got her pregnant and they moved away from the area on their own.

Residential vs. Institutional Care

Residential care programs are not just for teens in Denise's dire emotional circumstances. However, the sheer number of pregnant teens, complicated by lack of funds and space, often necessitates that those in greatest need are given first consideration.

Wendy's family of 12 children, with only their mother to support them, was one such case. Wendy's father had deserted the family a couple of years earlier, and, when Wendy got pregnant, her mother just did not have the financial resources to adequately provide for her own family, much less another child.

Wendy got into an institutional program for pregnant teens that proved to be a haven for the 14-year-old. She had the listening ear of good professionals, and continued her education while in the home.

The difference between residential and institutional programs is most often the number of girls living there during the pregnancy and post partum periods. Residential programs are likely to house 5 to 10 girls. Institutional programs house many more girls in a dormitory-type fashion. Every area of the country has completely different care offerings for pregnant teens. With the thousands of girls needing help, there are burgeoning pilot programs of all sorts. Contact your Social Service Agency, church, physician, and/or school guidance office for information on the programs in your area.

Wendy, like Denise, gave her baby up for adoption. Unlike Denise, Wendy had the advantage of a mother who welcomed her home with warm, loving arms. Wendy's counseling had helped her accept her father's desertion, as well as the family's poverty, and had also prepared her to aid her mother as best she could. Welfare and Aid to Dependent Children helped the family survive financially.

Happily, Wendy's experience with the program planted some hardy seeds of social conscience in her and, today, after working her way out of poverty, she herself is a marriage and family counselor. Wendy's mother now lives with one of her daughters. Those of her children who are able, contribute to her financial support.

Seeking Help from Other Family Members

Brenda's story is different from any of the others. She got pregnant at 17. Her father was very unhappy, but compassionate. Her mother, however, was irate and bitter. She resented Brenda to the point where she wasn't even civil to her. Brenda was so upset by her mother's rejection, as well as the severe strain she believed she had placed on her parents' relationship, that she started having trouble eating. Soon, she had lost several pounds, and her father became seriously concerned over her well-being. Unable to find even a small crack in his wife's armor of negative emotions, Brenda's father finally approached his sister and her husband, who lived several hundred miles away.

He explained the situation and asked if Brenda might live with them while she carried her pregnancy to term. It was anticipated that the baby would be given up for adoption. Brenda's aunt agreed that this was about the only acceptable choice for Brenda's sake. A week later, the girl flew the distance to be with her relatives.

After many days of much-needed space, Brenda's mother began coming out of her shock. She conceded that Brenda's pregnancy brought out emotional problems from deep within herself that she hadn't previously realized were so severe. Brenda's pregnancy had been the self-fulfillment of her mother's biggest fear—that she was not a good mother to Brenda. Brenda's parents began seeing a therapist together, and started solving some long-hidden problems.

As they collected themselves and Brenda's mother

began to feel as if she could face and deal with her daughter's pregnancy, word was received from Brenda's aunt that Brenda had lost her baby due to a premature birth. Brenda would be all right, but was very despondent.

If living away from home during a pregnancy is necessary for the physical or mental health of any member of the family, then this is, by far, preferable to living in hate, anger, or bitterness.

Brenda came home four days later. When she walked off the plane, she went immediately into her father's arms, sobbing. She ignored her mother completely. Brenda's father convinced Brenda to see the therapist with him and his wife and, over a period of several months, the family came to understand one another. They function happily today.

If living away from home during a pregnancy is necessary for the physical or mental health of any member of the family, then this is, by far, preferable to living in hate, anger, or bitterness.

May the Lord bless your efforts to find a satisfactory course of action to take with your pregnant teen. I trust the information in the following chapters may be useful for you, both in making your decision, and in living with it. Good luck!

S.O.S. #7

Are you being too hasty, pushy, and/or unrealistic

in trying to help your teen decide what to do about her pregnancy? If so, you may not be:

1. Listening to the teen's feelings, fears, wishes or ideas;
2. Seeing the reality of what the teen can or cannot deal with in choosing what to do about the pregnancy;
3. Dealing with what you, as a parent, can or cannot give to the situation in deciding what option to exercise now, and for the future;
4. Talking together at truly effective levels;
5. Drawing out her genuine, inner feelings about what she wants to do;
6. Seeing signs that will help lead you, as a family, to the right choice(s) for the pregnant teen;
7. Living by the direction given us in Colossians 3:17: *And whatever you do, whether in word or deed, do it all in the name of the Lord Jesus, giving thanks to God the Father through him.*

What Can You Do?

1. Slow down! Even if your teen is several weeks/months into her pregnancy, pushing or forcing the issues will do no good, and will only complicate things.
2. Honestly evaluate your teen's abilities, maturity and stamina. Think about how she reacts under ordinary pressures, such as tests in school, not being chosen for a class play, being asked to perform household chores, or other activities. By magnifying these many times over, you may glean an idea of what the pressures of parenthood could do to her.
3. Consider what your teen's relationship is with God. Does she easily put her trust in Him? Does she enjoy Jesus' presence as Saviour in her life?

4. How about you? List the things you have to give to the situation—physically, emotionally, financially and spiritually.
5. Practice asking your teen specific questions, then ponder her answers as you go about your day. Don't analyze to death what she says, but consider things that are out of character, inappropriately vehement and/or obviously inconsistent as areas where trouble is probably brewing.
6. Follow any hunches you may have and try to draw out her inner feelings by sharing other people's experiences. Items in the news media or local happenings may be helpful in discussions that might provide valuable clues to what your teen is feeling inside.
7. Suggest to your teen that she meet with a pastor, counselor, or other knowledgeable Christian with whom she feels comfortable to ask questions about God's commands, desires for her life, and what powers He gives her in order to live through crises.
8. Pray that you might, as James 1:19 says, *Be quick to listen, slow to speak and slow to become angry.*

S.O.S. #8

Have you considered the preciousness of life to God?

What Can You Do?

1. Read Jeremiah 1:4,5: *The word of the Lord came to me, saying, "Before I formed you in the womb I knew you, before you were born I set you apart; I appointed you as a prophet to the nations."*

2. Read the story of the Good Shepherd in John 10:7-18.

S.O.S. #9

In regard to marriage:

1. Does the teen feel she has a choice?
2. Do you feel you have a choice?
3. Do you trust that in all things God has a purpose for our good? Read Ecclesiastes 3:1-13.
4. Do you accept that, with choices, come certain consequences?
5. Are you taking your time, not rushing your teen into marriage?
6. Have you observed your teen and the boy she might marry together?
7. Are there any obvious areas of strain/differences in their relationship (for example, temperament, energy level, interests, priorities)?
8. Is your teen getting enough rest, proper nutrition, sound medical care?
9. Have you outlined in detail what you will and will not do for the teen couple in regard to finances, living arrangements, school, transportation, jobs, and babysitting if they do get married?
10. Are you using the dependency they have on you as power to control what they do, how they live?
11. Are you prepared to respect the teen couple's privacy and individualism?
12. Do they understand clearly that they must respect your privacy and possessions?
13. Have you discussed the need to be resilient, stressing that adversity enhances character and can also strengthen relationships?

14. Have you advised the couple on the importance of communication?
15. Have you told your teen there will be problems in the marriage relationship?
16. Have you emphasized the importance of living one day at a time?
17. Have you let the teen couple know about Jesus' waiting for them to let Him help them? Revelation 3:20 tells us, in Jesus' own words: *Here I am! I stand at the door and knock. If anyone hears my voice and opens the door, I will come in and eat with him, and he with me.*

What Can You Do?

1. Talk about any obvious personality differences that the teen couple has, and point out how these might cause problems in a marriage.
2. Get literature on the subject of health during pregnancy and encourage your teen to read it. Write down, together, a realistic plan for her diet and schedule.
3. Write down everything that pertains to how you will help the teen couple with housing and education. Put it in an agreement form, and have everyone involved sign it in good faith.
4. Honestly evaluate whether or not you are trying to control the situation and coerce the teens into doing what you want.
5. Develop a written work-to-earn agreement between you and the teens. Be specific about what the teens will receive for each job, including possible bonus programs for extra work and dock in pay for unperformed services.
6. Tell the teens about the sacredness of their relation-

ship as a couple, and that you wholly sanction this in marriage.

7. Good gifts for teens might include sound Christian books on the topics of marriage, sex, money, parenting, or handling adversity. An easy-to-understand version of the Bible is an invaluable offering to them.
8. Lead the teen couple to a premarital counseling session or program.
9. Remind the teens that Jesus came because God wants us all to live our lives to the full. Read John 10:10—Jesus tells us: *The thief comes only to steal and kill and destroy; I have come that they may have life, and have it to the full.*

S.O.S. #10

Think about the answers to the following questions:

1. Does your teen now know all the facts (and fantasies) about sex, birth control, disease, and responsibility?
2. Have you considered the main factors surrounding your daughter's pregnancy? Were there drugs/alcohol involved? How long has she dated her boyfriend? How old is she?
3. What does the father of your teen's baby feel about what to do?
4. What do his parents think?
5. In regard to helping your daughter to single-parent: Is there a great difference in how you, your spouse and/or daughter see the prospect?
6. Are there siblings' well-being to think about?
7. What are the money circumstances?
8. Are you trying to base your decisions with the well-

being of everyone in mind? First Corinthians 10:24 says: *Nobody should seek his own good, but the good of others.*

9. Have you let your teen voice her ideal scenario of what she wants to do?
10. Realistically, how much does your teen know about babies, cooking, cleaning, and finances?
11. Have you taken some time to put yourself in your teen's place?
12. Have you optimistically considered different choices and your part in each of them?
13. Have you verbally and emotionally recognized that your teen will be the mother of her baby and that you will respect her as such?
14. Are there special needs in your family, such as those concerning finances, illness, or physical handicaps? Contact your Social Service Agency.

What Can You Do?

1. If your teen doesn't know all the particulars of sex and birth control, discuss them with her now.
2. If you are unable to do so, get her a good Christian book on the subject. If she has questions, answer them, or get her to someone reliable who can.
3. Talk to your teen's boyfriend and his family. See how they view marriage and single parenting. Get a sense of their life-style and beliefs.
4. Discuss problem areas with your spouse, other children and pregnant teen. Have everyone write down what concerns them most. What would each like to see happen regarding the pregnancy?
5. Go to a professional care-giver if any area seems unresolvable.

6. Be very matter-of-fact about available and projected financial resources.
7. Ask God, in Jesus' name, to give you the strength to be unselfish and do what's right for the others involved.
8. Have your teen write down what she would do if she could have things exactly as she wishes.
9. Call your County Extension Service or Social Service Department and ask if they have any pamphlets about parenting or homemaking. Check your public/church libraries for useful aids in these areas.
10. Exercise your memory. Think back to when you were a teenager, a new bride/groom, a new parent. Share some of these memories with your teen.
11. When the situation seems too much to bear, remember Isaiah 40:31: *But those who hope in the Lord will renew their strength. They will soar on wings like eagles; they will run and not grow weary, they will walk and not be faint.*
12. Write down the ground rules for a single parent arrangement in your family. All those involved should sign the agreement.
13. Be sure to discuss the basics of the relationship you, as a grandparent, will have with the new baby and its teen mother.

S.O.S. #11

When your family is considering adoption, have you thought about:

1. The effects it might have on each member of the family?
2. That adoption inherently has many painful aspects?

3. The advice of your family doctor, a social worker, adoption agent, attorney, counselor, and/or pastor?
4. What God wants you to do? Pray, talk to trusted friends and family members and trained professionals in searching for this answer!
5. Your teen's personality?
6. That adoption is irrevocable?
7. That, if you don't agree with your teen's decision, she still needs your support, even if you cannot give your approval?
8. That there are numerous ways to arrange an adoption, and that, in talking to several people/agencies, you will be better prepared to find the right way for your family?

What Can You Do?

1. When adoption is being considered, there are very real benefits in talking to professionals, such as counselors, social workers, pastors, attorneys, and adoption agency caseworkers. Do not hesitate to seek all the help you need in sorting through this choice.
2. Ask each family member what his/her feelings are in regard to an adoption. This is vital! For instance, a younger son may wonder, "If my sister can give a baby away because she doesn't want it, will Mom/Dad give me away someday?" Clarify what is going on.
3. Face the fact that this will have painful effects. Confess your heartache to God, asking for His guidance and strength.
4. Know that, to adopting parents, a child is one of the most precious blessings in the world. They receive a child into their lives with the same sense of love, responsibility, and fulfillment as do biological parents.

S.O.S. #12

Is having your teen live away from home the best solution under your individual circumstances?

What Can You Do?

Read the story of the prodigal son in Luke 15:11-32 as a family. Pray together that your teen, having been away from home under her own trying conditions, will be received lovingly and gratefully back into your midst. Assure her that you will rejoice upon her return home!

Our Hand in His

Answering the following questions may help you gain an overall view of your feelings in trying to decide what is best for your pregnant teen. It may also guide a professional along in working through problems with you about the decisions you will make, or have already made.

1. Are you trying to rush your teen into any choices regarding her pregnancy and future?
2. Have you thought about the factors that contributed to your daughter's pregnancy?
3. While trying to decide what course of action should be taken regarding your teen's pregnancy, have you carefully considered her personality?
4. Are you honestly considering what you can and cannot give to help your daughter?
5. Is the situation adding so much strain on family relationships, or is it so overwhelming, that you are leaning toward such a decision as abortion in order to be

rid of the problem? (If you are: get professional help immediately.)

6. Are you talking about the pregnancy, and are all those involved expressing their feelings openly?
7. Are everyone's feelings being respected?
8. Do you sense that your daughter's true, inner feelings are different from those being expressed?
9. Are you discussing options according to what is really right for your family, or are things being decided in a flow of what others think should be done?
10. Are you praying together as a family?
11. Are you thinking about and listening for what God wants you to do?
12. Are you trying to think ahead to the consequences of what the future may hold for your teen, depending on the decisions you help her make now?
13. Is there a part of you that may be trying to punish yourself, your spouse or your daughter through what course of action is taken now?
14. Are you letting history repeat itself, living in a pattern that is not healthy or necessary, taking the easy way out, and/or trying to take control of issues that are not innately yours to control?
15. Is the pregnancy looked upon as a punishment from God?
16. Have you considered Romans 10:9,10? Is this how you are approaching the issue of your teen's pregnancy?
17. Have you straightened out any misconceptions your teen may have about God's capacity to forgive and help? Romans 3:22-24 says: *This righteousness from God comes through faith in Jesus Christ to all who believe. There is no difference, for all have sinned and fall short of the glory of God, and are justified freely by*

his grace through the redemption that came by Christ Jesus.

18. What is the teen's relationship to the father of her child? What is yours?
19. How about the relationship with his parents?
20. Are your family's beliefs and life-styles compatible with theirs?
21. How much does your teen know about orchestrating family life?
22. Have you shared your memories, pain, and disappointment with your family?
23. If the baby will remain with the teen through marriage or single parenting, have you determined to let your teen do the parenting?
24. Have you contacted sources of help for any special needs your family may have?
25. If you are considering adoption, have all family members communicated their thoughts freely in regard to how they feel about it?
26. Have you considered the precious gift that a child is to adoptive parents?
27. Are you unable to handle the pregnancy to the point that it might be better if your teen lived away from home for a period of time?
28. Have you given your greatest thoughts and efforts in working toward solutions to the problems surrounding your teen's pregnancy?

CHAPTER FOUR

Coping with the Pregnancy and Birth

For the pregnant teen who is in junior high or high school, ongoing education is a very important issue for several reasons. One is continuity. Everything else in her life is in upheaval—her feelings, physical condition, and relationships. The continuity of school is highly desirable. If she can continue attending classes in the same environment, at least in the first months of the pregnancy, it is ideal.

If this is not feasible because of school policy, physical symptoms, or the fact that she is unable emotionally to cope with facing her teachers and peers on a daily basis, then explore alternatives. Inquire with a school guidance or career counselor about adult education programs offered by the public school, a local vocational college, or other educational institutions in your area.

A new learning environment can be somewhat unsettling to the young teen, but it will fulfill a second reason for the importance of her education—contact with other people. It is imperative that a pregnant teen not be isolated from the social mainstream.

DANGERS OF ISOLATION

Gena, whose family was disrupted and ashamed over her pregnancy at 15, was taken out of public school. Her parents acted rashly, out of their neurotic need to try to hide Gena's condition from the world.

After several weeks of being home alone day after day, Gena changed from a spunky, elfin teenager into a frumpy, soap opera addict. She gained extra weight, became sullen, and lost any motivation she may have had to hope and plan for a bright future.

As Gena's pregnancy progressed, she hungered more and more for human contact outside her family. Sporadically, she would call one or another of her girlfriends in the evening, only to be driven further into depression by their tales of school and social happenings.

One horrifying conversation brought Gena to deep despair. A friend told her that the boy who had fathered Gena's baby was now going steady with another girl in their ninth grade class. This girl was a cheerleader, honor roll student, cute, and popular. Hearing of this girl's association with the boy who had rejected Gena as soon as he knew of her pregnancy was the epitome of humiliation for Gena.

Shortly after hanging up the phone, Gena said good night to her parents, went upstairs to her bathroom, and swallowed an entire bottle of aspirin. Fortunately, Gena's mother went to check on her daughter before retiring for the night. Seeing Gena lying near the bathtub, unmoving, she called the paramedics immediately. An ambulance delivered Gena to the intensive care unit of the local hospital where she lay for five days, barely holding onto her life. Her baby was prematurely stillborn. At a turning point in her recovery, a psychiatrist gave Gena his word that he would see her through her pain if only she would choose to live. From this time on, Gena's condition improved.

People need people. God mandates this repeatedly throughout the Scriptures. To isolate a young, pregnant girl is a heinous injustice to her well-being.

Gena's parents are not bad people who wished their daughter harm. But, as countless others involved in any number of tragic situations, their inability to face, cope with, and ask for help regarding their problems contributed to a senseless, sorrowful loss.

This kind of situation is a poignant statement about our need to share and acknowledge one another's burdens in life (see 1 Corinthians 12:12-26).

THE NEED FOR HUMAN GROUNDING

God recognizes each one of us with perfectly equal love and concern. We must put one another's needs into our line of vision, and intertwine our Christian resources to help buoy the hurting souls that surround us. Connecting with one another is absolutely essential to our survival and salvation. Hebrews 3:13 tells us: *But encourage one another daily, as long as it is called Today, so that none of you may be hardened by sin's deceitfulness.*

Pregnant teenagers are no exception. If there are no educational programs in your area (this would be extremely rare), then, at the very least, check on the possibilities of obtaining a tutor. Again, call the public school(s) in your area. Tell them it is imperative that you find educational help for a pregnant teen, and that you need assistance in doing so. Keep contacting people/agencies until you find someone who can lead you to a workable solution. Pastors, counselors, social service agencies, or teachers are all dependable sources of information.

More than classroom skills, then, it is *human grounding* that a pregnant teen needs. She has to derive some form of nourishment for her self-esteem. Whether this is found through a school she is used to attending, a new classroom group comprised of other students having special needs, or a one-to-one connection with a tutor, a young girl's sense of emotional perspective depends largely on having others around her, and on an ongoing learning experience.

STUDYING FOR THE FUTURE

Which brings us to the third reason why continuing an education is important for a pregnant teen—ongoing learning. For many girls who are pregnant, a common course of action has been, and, to some extent, still is: to quit school, get married, have a baby, raise a family and/or be stuck in a low-paying, laboring job position. This is not to imply that there is anything wrong with laboring jobs. There is not. What may be wrong is when a would-be medical researcher finds herself working as a gas station attendant because she hasn't learned any specialized job skills. This young woman may have little hope of getting the formal education she needs to become a medical researcher.

Whether married or a single parent, experiencing

some kind of ongoing learning is essential to developing several life skills. Some of them are: self-motivation, maintaining a schedule, self-discipline, mental stimulation, keeping a healthy perspective (and not having time to sink into self-pity), feeding self-esteem, and developing a sense of direction for the future.

This does not mean a young girl should establish a firm career goal prematurely, but that she at least grasp a sense of going forward, rather than backward, on her life's path. It is true that, with enough single steps, a person can journey almost anywhere. Giving a teen this kind of optimistic attitude may be the single most notable ingredient to bolster her spirits throughout an incredibly formidable challenge in her life.

TAKING ADVANTAGE OF OPPORTUNITIES

For the girl who does quit regular school, there is another way to complete her high school education and to start accomplishing the development of the life skills listed. This consists of a brief period of study to pass an exam for high school proficiency, which, in most cases, results in the receipt of a High School Equivalency (or General Education) Diploma. Check with the public school in your town for information on how your state educational system provides this service.

In this circumstance, the teen may not be in a long-term classroom situation, but she is working toward something positive, and experiences the fulfilling reward of reaching an admirable goal when she is done. Finishing anything, whether it is a thesis or a high school proficiency test, is rewarding in its own right.

Leslie was a pregnant 18-year-old who got married and was determined that she would complete her high school education in this manner. She attended a class one evening a week for eight weeks. Then, passing her high school proficiency test with honorably high scores, she was able to participate in her former high school class's commencement exercises.

Leslie received her diploma (issued from the State Board of Education and mailed to her high school's principal) with her classmates. Leslie's parents, in-laws, and husband sat proudly in the audience with her new baby son.

This achievement gave Leslie such encouragement that, after graduation and spending the summer getting acquainted with motherhood, she enrolled in fall classes at a local junior college two nights a week to learn bookkeeping skills.

Leslie now enjoys performing related services for several clients from her home base and contributes an impressive amount of income to the family finances, while simultaneously orchestrating household demands and caring for her son.

Her self-motivation and enthusiasm rubbed off on her young husband, He, in turn, attended classes one night a week at the same college, learning more about his field of work as an apprentice electrician in order to increase his value within the company he works for and to prepare to have a business of his own some day.

PURSUING A LIFE EDUCATION

Life education is a process that is never complete. However, if this process is hindered because of a teen pregnancy, its lessons and, particularly, its benefits can become warped to the point of negating the positive effects of both school and life education.

Having hope for a better tomorrow can be an avenue for, and enhance the momentum of, a pregnant teen's mental health into a productive, effective, and successful life-education experience.

Sandy, pregnant at 14, dropped out of school after the eighth grade. With no real support network at her disposal, she became merely a reflection of the healthy teen she had been. After the birth of her baby, Sandy worked as a cashier in a convenience store at night, while she hired a former classmate to baby-sit. This turned out to be an undependable situation. When the friend could not sit, Sandy had to call into work *sick,* having no one else she could trust with the baby. With one poor job after another, one inadequate baby-sitter after the other, and growing financial problems, Sandy's small emotional reserve of hope was soon depleted. Her life education had inevitably continued—it continued to embitter and exhaust her. The dreams and ideals of a bright future, which most teens carry into their 20s, were arrested for Sandy before she ever got to high school.

Parents, counselors, educators—try to help a teen receive the best ongoing learning experience possible in her individual circumstances. Having hope for a better tomorrow can be an avenue for, and enhance the momentum of, a pregnant teen's mental health into a productive, effective, and successful life-education experience.

Bear in mind the assurance in Romans 5:5: *Hope does not disappoint us, because God has poured out his love into our hearts by the Holy Spirit, whom he has given us.*

DEALING WITH RESENTMENTS

Pam, 17, was already eight months pregnant when her father, Don, finally blew up. "I can't take this any more!" he shouted one morning. He promptly marched downstairs and approached his wife. "Barb, I have to do something! I can't handle this thing with Pam! Every time I look at her, all I see is her stomach! I want to strangle her—and that brat who got her pregnant!"

Barb was acutely aware of the frustration that had been building within Don for weeks. His repulsion toward Pam seemed to have grown in direct proportion to Pam's expanding midsection. Now, she laid a hand gently on Don's arm. "Honey, I think you should see a therapist before this gets totally out of control."

Don agreed that this would be the healthiest approach in trying to resolve his destructive feelings. He went to a marriage and family counselor who had a Christian background.

Don expressed great guilt over his repulsion toward Pam. The counselor calmly pointed out that Don needn't feel guilty over his feelings. "Feelings are not sinful. They have no *good* or *bad* rating, they simply exist. If you feel repulsion toward Pam in her pregnant condition, that's just the way it is. Sin comes into play when we *act* on our feelings in a hateful or vengeful way. If you were to physically or emotionally abuse Pam in expressing your negative feelings, Don, then you would be disobeying God's will.

"Ephesians 4:26 tells us, *In your anger do not sin.* This clearly indicates that it is not the feeling, but the action that is wrong.

"What we need to do, Don, is help you find a way to either accept your feelings and let time pass, or change them."

Don nodded in understanding. "But I don't know how to do either of those!"

"Well, Don," the counselor responded, "first I'd like to try to clean out some cobwebs with you. I would like to help guide you toward the fulfillment of 2 Corinthians 5:17 in your life, which says: *Therefore, if anyone is in Christ, he is a new creation; the old is gone, the new has come!*

"I have a suspicion that there are some old influences in your life that may be preventing you from getting to the new, more understanding you.

"Can you identify anything that may have happened to you as a child or young adult that might be a root cause for your reactions to Pam now?"

Finding Reasons Behind Resentments

As Don was counseled over the next several weeks, an unraveling of some very interesting events in his life shed much needed light on why Don had reacted as he did toward Pam.

First, it became apparent that Don's own childhood had been riddled with tension. The oldest of three children, he was intensely jealous after his first younger sibling was born. This was expressed in angry, resentful acts during his mother's next pregnancy, when Don would hit at the baby in his mother's growing abdomen and tell her to "send it back!"

Don was five at the time, and his sister was three. He lived out his resentment for her by pulling her hair, shoving her to the ground during play, and crying to his mother that he didn't want another one like her.

Don's mother, feeling guilty over her son's disturbance, compounded the problem by showering Don with increased but misdirected love and affection. She told him what a wonderful child he was, and openly rejected her toddler daughter at times in front of Don to show him how important he was, thinking that her daughter was too young to be affected by the situation.

Don learned that, to get his mother's pampering and affection, all he had to do was act mean and cantankerous. However, he instinctively knew that something was wrong with this chain of interactions. Therefore, he felt increasingly apprehensive and confused. In his child's version of guilt, Don reacted by becoming more demanding. This was his way of begging his mother to set things right in his world. Unfortunately, this never happened and, in order to survive psychologically, Don tucked his feelings away into his subconscious *memory tapes*.

When his own teenage daughter became pregnant, before Don was ready to give her up to someone else's love and affection, these old tapes automatically began to play again in his mind. Consequently, Don's responsive feelings toward Pam became a mixture of those he'd had toward his pregnant mother, his younger sibling, and his own feelings as a child. Discovering this as an adult, nearly 40 years after the fact, was a complete surprise to Don's grown-up mental consciousness.

Once he was able to recognize the reasons for his feelings and put away the childish fears and guilt of his past, he began to cope with these same feelings as a man.

First Corinthians 13:11 says: *When I was a child, I talked like a child, I thought like a child, I reasoned like a child. When I became a man, I put childish ways behind me.*

It is, of course, perfectly understandable that a person carries some childish ways into his adulthood. However, each Christian is responsible to mature in his life. It is up to the individual, as old mental tapes play in his current life, to seek out God's will for his new, grown-up self, and

If you have no distinct pattern of past problems that may be prompting feelings of frustration, resentment, or repulsion with your teen, search your memory for the types of input and experiences you have had with the subject of pregnant teenagers.

to put his childhood behind him.

Most often, when a new situation presents itself to an unprepared adult (and having a pregnant teenager is most certainly one of these situations), the adult reacts in a way that his brain is most nearly familiar with. If there is no root for the reaction in his past, then the brain *makes up* a reaction, according to what input it has received over many months or years in regard to the situation.

Therefore, if you have no distinct pattern of past problems that may be prompting feelings of frustration, resentment, or repulsion with your teen, search your memory for the types of input and experiences you have had with the subject of pregnant teenagers.

Have any movies, articles, statistical reports, seminars, or news presentations influenced your feelings? Are your feelings founded in a conscious, thoughtful, and legitimate basis? Or are you on automatic pilot, reacting according to how you think you should react? Patiently remind yourself to put away the old and let the new begin to seep through into your attitude.

Some Honest Communication

A second tape was playing in Don's mind and causing him trouble in a different area. He was most put off by what he saw as Pam's laziness as her pregnancy progressed.

Don found that this antagonized him to the point of having to strain to hold back his anger at her. Pam was not cleaning her room, helping around the house, or keeping up with her studies. Don mostly blamed Barb for this. He told his counselor, "Barb is home all day. She should be supervising Pam and making sure she carries out her responsibilities!"

"And so there's a strain between you and Barb over how she is dealing with Pam and the pregnancy?"

"Yes," Don acknowledged.

"Do you think Barb would come for a couple of our sessions? Or would that make you uncomfortable, Don?"

"No," Don said, "it wouldn't make me uncomfortable, and yes, I think Barb would come."

She did. The three discussed the situation and the problems brewing at home. Barb felt that it was her maternal duty to do all she could to make Pam's life easier in her time of need. Barb and Don communicated back and forth on this topic extensively. Barb discovered that she was actually being a crutch for Pam; the more she did for Pam, the less Pam felt she was able to do for herself.

Barb also discussed a sibling rivalry she had watched develop between Pam and her younger brothers.

Pam's anxiety over the pregnancy, approaching birth, and her future as a parent was causing her to be more competitive for her mother's attention, which gave the girl a sense of comfort.

The boys, however, felt they were losing Barb's affection and became very possessive of her. Barb felt torn between her children's needs. To try to compensate, she had channeled more of her energy into parenting and less into her marriage.

Don felt that Barb's concentrated efforts had been the cause of a wall that appeared to be building between him and the other family members.

Barb, on the other hand, felt that Don had purposely withdrawn his emotional support when Pam's pregnancy began to physically show. She was only now beginning to absorb how much Don's childhood experiences had affected him. Her resentment toward Don, thinking he had left her emotionally in the lurch to run the family alone, was causing Barb great discomfort.

As the couple opened up to each other more and more, they were able to adjust to each other's feelings and expectations. The counselor gently directed their conversations during the weekly sessions. This practice gave the couple enough momentum and know-how to carry through on the methods at home with each other.

Breaking Through to God's Peace

At times, it was very difficult to remain calm. As new layers of emotions were exposed in one or the other, Barb and Don sometimes found themselves in the midst of unexpected turmoil and intense reaction. There were angry outbursts, bitter confrontations, and many tears. The couple tried to back away when these emotions erupted. They made every effort to stop themselves, confess and apologize for any unfair accusations, and then go about their separate activities until they could come back to the conversation later when they had both settled down.

Don and Barb put their faith in their heavenly Father.

They prayed that, just as Jesus was able to calm the sea in Matthew 8:23-27, so God would help them calm their turbulent feelings in order that they could effectively grow toward a fuller, stronger relationship.

There are many unpleasant feelings and reactions that can surface with a pregnant teenager in your life. Taken by surprise, it can be a great temptation to try to ignore and stuff these unanticipated feelings deep down inside, rather than confronting and dealing with them. But beware! This can be like packing a charge into a stick of dynamite and risking detonation at some unknown time and place. Much better to face and work through problems as they arise, and either accept or change them.

CHILD'S BODY PUSHED INTO ADULTHOOD

When a young girl gets pregnant, her body is obviously able to accommodate new life. This does not mean her body is ready to support a baby. A teen is still growing. A pregnancy causes certain levels of strain on the development of every cell in her body. Energy that would normally go into the growth of her own bones, tissue, and mental development is now shared in helping her unborn child develop.

One area that is heavily affected is the endocrine system. Hormone levels, which have been rumbling along the changing path of adolescence, are suddenly thrown into total diversion. A child's body unexpectedly requires the estrogen and progesterone levels of an adult!

Feeling the Physical Strain

Sixteen-year-old Kathy was seven months into her pregnancy. A typical teen, mad-dashing here and there for any number of activities, she had been feeling somewhat overtired for a week or two. Her back and joints were a little achy. Dark circles were becoming prominent under her eyes.

One morning, Kathy tried to get out of bed, but simply couldn't bring herself to do it. Her mind seemed dull. When she didn't come to the table for breakfast, her mother went to check on her.

"Mom, I must have the flu or something," Kathy mumbled, and rolled over. She slept well into the afternoon.

Concerned, her mother woke her up to give her some tea and check her temperature. There was no fever, nor any other signs of a virus or infection. Barely able to stay awake long enough to drink down the tea, Kathy went back to sleep until late the next morning.

When her mother brought her a tray with a light breakfast, Kathy refused to eat, insisting groggily that she just wanted to sleep. Worried now, Kathy's mother called the doctor, who assured her that Kathy probably had a little bug. He said to let her sleep it off, if that's what her body was telling her to do.

Kathy slept another 24 hours. She only got up to go to the bathroom. When she did this, her mother would get her to drink a glass of juice. Another 24 hours passed, and Kathy's mother called the doctor again. This time he was perplexed. Having been Kathy's doctor since birth, the doctor readily offered to make a house call on his way home from his office.

After checking Kathy's vital signs, the baby's heartbeat, and examining Kathy, the doctor's diagnosis was sure. "She's just plain exhausted. Her mind and body have been so called upon that she's subconsciously shut down for a few days. I'd wager she'll be up and around sometime tomorrow."

She was. Kathy ate a light lunch the following day, took a shower, and read quietly for the afternoon. Her mind cleared and, in a few days, she felt fine.

The body and mind are wondrous, miraculous teammates. Working hand-in-hand from the moment of existence, there is no real separation of one from the other. If one is out of sync, the other will be, also.

Response in a pregnant teen can be pronounced, as it was in Kathy, to the point of extreme. The body and mind will do what has to be done to preserve life—in Kathy's case, both hers and her baby's.

After this frightening episode, Kathy's mother was much more conscientious about helping Kathy pace herself. Kathy was more careful to take her prenatal vitamins each morning; eat several small, nutritious meals every day; take a period of quiet and rest in the afternoons; and take a solitary walk in the early evenings. The last eight weeks of her pregnancy were free from trouble.

When Kathy went to the hospital with labor pains, she had good color, felt strong, and had the muscle tone desirable for a safe birth. Her new son was healthy, alert, and of average weight.

Emotional Effects

Jordan, 17, seemed to sail through her pregnancy with ease. She wasn't ill for even a day. The wear on her body manifested itself more in the emotional realm. She was so moody that her parents were at a loss as to how to interact with her on any sort of consistent basis. One day she was teary, depressed, and anxious. The next she was cold, aloof, and sarcastic. The teeming activity within Jordan's mind and body, which, of course, no one could actually see, played havoc with her response to the outside world.

Roller-coaster hormone levels and chemical imbalances can cause a nightmare of confusion and fear for the pregnant teen.

Jordan was also deeply concerned about the stretch marks that appeared on her body as she became heavy with child. Her breasts, stomach, inner thighs, and hips were covered with purple and white lines that looked somewhat like the tributaries of a river on a map. To her, these marks were hideous and ugly. She informed her mother that she would never be able to wear a bikini again, and that no man could ever love her with such a reminder of her past.

Jordan's mother pooh-poohed her daughter's concern, and chastised her for worrying over such a vain thing.

However, what Jordan's mother did not realize or even stop to consider was that, to a blossoming young woman, things like stretch marks are very important, even disabling, to self-esteem, not necessarily because of vanity, but for more basic, underlying reasons.

Fortunately, Jordan's female gynecologist was perceptive and understanding about such things. At a checkup where Jordan bemoaned her upset over the physical scars of her pregnancy, Dr. Logan reassured her gently. "I know, Jordan. Your stretch marks are a constant physical reminder to you that your pregnancy has totally disrupted your youth.

"You see, psychologically, they are also like a horrible case of acne, and they eat at your self-esteem. This is because teenagers are not naturally comfortable enough with themselves to easily accept physical imperfections. Don't feel too badly about your anxiety over them. Stretch marks bother even some of the most confident women I know.

"Emotionally, you need to know two main things. One is that older women get stretch marks, too. They are not a curse placed on pregnant teenagers. They discriminate only among skin types, not age groups. Some people's skin is simply more elastic than others.

"Second, stretch marks do not make you unlovable to a man! A man who is so adversely affected by any superficial scarring has an emotional problem in some area of his own life, possibly in getting beyond the surface of a relationship to a level of deeper bonding and intimacy.

"Perfection does not exist, Jordan. As a teenager, it is highly possible that you have not matured enough to discern between the romantic propaganda of artificial beauty and the reality that beauty is actually generated from within loving, well-adjusted people."

Jordan felt much better after this consultation with Dr. Logan, whom she considered to be a beautiful woman in her own right. And Jordan was bright enough to identify with the fact that beauty truly does come from within. Dr. Logan's sparkling eyes and dancing smile attested to that.

The doctor also had noted a Scripture for Jordan to look up—Proverbs 31:30: *Charm is deceptive, and beauty is fleeting; but a woman who fears the Lord is to be praised.*

Aftereffects

After Jordan gave birth to an eight-pound baby girl, she discovered that the pregnancy had taken quite a toll on her physically, much beyond the stretch marks.

Almost immediately, even though Jordan had been given shots to dry up her breast milk (since she was not nursing), her breasts became filled with milk anyway. This caused two days of great pain and discomfort.

Within the next several weeks, Jordan had problems with infection in the area of stitches from her episiotomy; discomfort from hemorrhoids; difficulty in controlling her bowel movements because of a torn rectal wall; a nagging backache that eventually X-rays revealed was caused by Jordan's maturing hip bones not having gone back into place following the delivery of her daughter; and Jordan's dental health had suffered severely—not having had one cavity before, she now had eleven!

Certainly, any of these medical issues can affect new mothers, regardless of age, but it is only natural that a developing teenager is more vulnerable to them in the first place, often to a greater degree.

A young woman's body being pushed prematurely into adulthood is a serious matter. As such, it deserves the care and attention required to prevent as much permanent damage to her overall health as possible. Proper rest, diet, and exercise plans should be carefully followed.

WHO'S FOOTING THE BILL?

Bev North, a financial aid counselor, sat with 15-year-old Tricia and her mother, Mary, in Bev's office at the county's Social Services Department. Tricia was three months pregnant and anticipated keeping her baby. Mary, a single working parent, supported Tricia and her two younger sisters. Tricia's father lived out of the area and only saw his daughters on special occasions throughout the year. Worried over medical costs, Mary had contacted Bev several days earlier.

Bev explained, "There are several financial options to review in regard to pregnant teenagers. I would like to mention each to see which ones might apply to your circumstances.

Private Health Insurance

"First, and ideally, there is private health insurance coverage. Mary, do you have a private or group health care policy?"

"Yes," Mary said, "through my job. But it only covers me. Since my divorce, the girls' father, Carl, has had responsibility for their health insurance coverage."

"Okay," Bev said, writing something on a pad of paper, "then we need to see if Carl's health insurance covers a minor daughter's pregnancy."

"We already checked," Mary replied. "The policy he carries on the girls will only cover sick or injury expenses. It does not cover well-care, such as normal maternity benefits.

"For instance, if Tricia required a caesarean delivery or had complications after a natural birth, they would pay. But not for any usual prenatal, delivery, or postpartum expenses.

"And they wouldn't pick up the baby's expenses under any circumstances."

"I see." Bev tapped the eraser end of her pencil against her lip. "Well, then, what about the baby's father's parents? Is it possible that they have a more comprehensive policy that would help out?"

"Only if we got married," Tricia answered quietly. "Then his father's group policy would pick up 80 per cent of everything."

Social Service Funds and Other Programs

"Okay." Bev laid down her pencil. "It looks like we'd better get some financial aid forms and see what benefits, if any, you might qualify for from the county or state Social Service Funds."

As it turned out, Mary, having custody and responsibility for her minor daughters but receiving financial support from Carl, made too much money to receive any aid from Social Service Funds. She would only be eligible for indigent patient funds in the event that there was an unforseeable problem, just short of a catastrophe, with Tricia or her baby.

Mary was incredulous. "I can't believe this! Why, I'm just able to make ends meet, and the guidelines say I make too much money! This is ridiculous!"

"I know," Bev said, "it seems terribly unfair. Each state is different, and counties within states can also offer various programs. There are some states that offer a kind of medical care program that approaches socialized medicine benefits for lower-middle and middle income families.

"Unfortunately, we don't have anything like that. If we just can't find another way to work this out, is there any possibility that you have friends or family who live near a university hospital or medical research facility? Sometimes, there are programs through such institutions that might offer aid to girls in Tricia's circumstances."

Mary was adamant. "No! We're in this as a family, and we'll have to find a way right here."

Private Arrangements

Bev nodded. "All right. Then let's contemplate. Assuming a normal pregnancy, birth, and postpartum, how can we go about working out a program of payments with Tricia's doctor, the hospital, and pediatrician for the new baby?

"With an older, low-risk mother, I might suggest using a midwife and having a home delivery but, at Tricia's young age, I think it is wisest to stick with hospital methods for safety's sake."

"Yes," Mary agreed, "and our doctor is in family practice, so he's in a position to care for Tricia, deliver and care for the baby. So, primarily, we need to contact the doctor and the hospital to arrange for payments."

Supplemental Assistance

Bev went on to the next issue. "Well, then, we will need to concern ourselves with preparation for after the baby's birth. If Tricia is going to live on her own with the child, then, more than likely, she will qualify for some sort of combination of welfare and Aid to Dependent Children (ADC) benefits. If she continues to live with you, ADC might be the program to investigate for her.

"Will the baby's father acknowledge or assume any responsibility?"

"I'm not sure," Tricia answered.

"Well, then," Bev said, reaching for a business card at the front of her desk, "I'm going to give you this phone number for the Legal Aid Office. You need to contact an attorney there who will help you. His fees will be on a free or sliding basis within your ability to pay according to their scales.

"It is essential that you determine your legal rights. The baby's father might have an obligation to help you support the child—sometimes, to the point where the District Attorney's office arranges to garnish his wages, if he has any, and if necessary."

Creative Finance

In the end, Mary arranged to pay the doctor $50 each month throughout Tricia's pregnancy and after the baby's birth until the account was current. There would be no finance charges added to this.

Living in a small city, there was only one hospital, which demanded half of the anticipated costs before they would admit a noninsured patient such as Tricia; the balance of her bill would have to be paid before she would be discharged. There was no way for Mary to pay these lump sums, so Carl, Tricia's father, agreed to borrow the money from a commercial lender in his area. Tricia would make half of the monthly payments to Carl once the baby was two months old and she could get a part-time job. Carl would contribute the other $50 a month as his way of helping Tricia, and would cover the full payments the first two to four months.

It was decided that Tricia would continue living at home with her mother and sisters and her baby. She would apply for ADC for supplemental support for the baby if her search through the legal system was fruitless regarding help from the baby's father, since the young man and his parents refused to have anything to do with Tricia or the baby.

Seek Necessary Help

Balancing financial demands with physical and mental needs can be very difficult. But with a loving, supportive family, creative planning, and cooperation it can all be accomplished.

Maybe your family is fortunate enough to have health insurance coverage for medical costs, or you otherwise have the cash available to pay the expenses for your pregnant teen. If so, keep a special place in your heart and prayers for the many thousands of families who don't. Their financial struggles can be excruciatingly painful at times.

If you are in the midst of financial pressures, trying to work out a plan of action for (and with) your pregnant teen, be realistic and flexible. As you have read here, there is a wide variety of possibilities in regard to finances and how to fulfill these needs. From one geographical area to another, there are different programs in effect for aid. No two doctors, hospitals, funding programs, health insurance policies, or personal bank accounts are exactly alike. Exhaust every avenue available in your circumstances in order to plot the best financial course for yourself and your teen.

A caution in regard to financial aid—if you need it, do not be ashamed to get it! Money can be a very sensitive subject, especially in today's fast-paced, materialistic society. Don't let your pride about money stand in the way of filling real needs—yours, your teen's, or her baby's.

When considering your individual financial responsibilities as a Christian, and in avoiding prideful decisions, bear in mind that it is not money itself that causes us problems. Rather, it is the *love of money* (see 1 Tim. 6:10) that can prompt much heartache and separation from God.

Pray that you might be guided with a humble spirit to make the right decisions in regard to your pregnant teen and money. Ask God, in Jesus' name, to help you find the strength to put false pride away from you and to seek financial help if you need it.

THE BIRTH, POSTPARTUM, AND HOMECOMING

Peg woke up on a weekday morning feeling crampy, almost as though she were going to start a period. Her lower back and legs ached slightly. As she stretched in her first waking moments, she thought, "Oh brother, just what I need—some weird virus!"

When Peg went to the bathroom, however, she was filled with panic to see a pinkish stain on her underpants. She immediately called to her mother.

Facing Reality

Marge Dobbs smiled knowingly as Peg told her of the stain and physical discomfort she was experiencing. She said,

They knew there was no way to insulate her from the demands of parenthood or the problems of still having to grow up herself while trying to raise a baby.

"Peg, I think you'll be a mom before this time tomorrow!"

Peg's mouth dropped open. Of course, she knew the birth was imminent, but it had not seemed a reality—more like something of a dream into the future, like the time she had anticipated her first jet airplane ride, but hadn't really been able to imagine the butterflies that had filled her stomach as the engines roared in preparation for takeoff.

Marge put her arm around her daughter's shoulders. "Don't be so surprised, Peg. Your due date is only a week away!"

"I know, Mom," Peg answered, swallowing visibly. "But somehow I don't feel ready."

"You can't really be ready for the experience of childbirth, Peg. There are no words to actually describe it, no matter how many children you have. Each new life comes into this world in its own unique way."

"But, Mom," Peg's voice was shaky, "I'm scared. I didn't think I would be."

Marge hugged her daughter tightly. "Just try to concentrate on this, honey—regardless of any pain, fear, or exhaustion, millions of women go through childbirth every year, and they come through on the other side just fine."

Waiting Out the Labor

Marge planned to go to the hospital with Peg, whose boyfriend had left the scene as soon as he heard of the pregnancy. It had taken Peg about three months to get over that hurt. Marge knew there were inner wounds from the rejection that were still healing, and she hoped they wouldn't be ripped open with the pressures a newborn would bring to Peg's life. She also hoped there would not be scars to cause Peg much trouble in future relationships. Marge and her husband, Jim, were trying very hard to help Peg through the trauma of teenage pregnancy, but they knew there was no way to insulate her from the demands of parenthood or the problems of still having to grow up herself while trying to raise a baby.

Marge would be in the delivery room with Peg, but Jim would not. Both he and Peg were uncomfortable with that, and Jim opted to wait at home with their other daughter and son for news of his first grandchild's arrival.

Peg went through the day at a slow but apprehensive pace. As dinner time neared that evening, she began grasping at her lower back every half an hour or so. Marge watched carefully, but did not make a big deal about how smooth and relatively quickly the labor seemed to be progressing. About eight that evening, Peg's pains were coming twenty minutes apart, each lasting a couple of minutes. A call to the doctor brought a hearty response. "Well,

well," he chuckled, "so, Peg's going to cost me a good night's sleep! Probably won't deliver until the wee hours of the morning. Just for precaution, however, we'd better check her in within the hour. You never know with a first baby, especially when Mom is a teenager!"

It's Time

Shortly after one in the morning, the floor nurse called the doctor from the lounge where he'd been napping off and on during the evening. "It's time," she told him over the phone. "She's ready."

The medical team moved into quick, efficient action. Marge scrubbed and gowned. She walked behind the nurse, who pushed Peg along on the gurney toward the delivery room. Peg cried, "Mom! Mom, where are you?"

"I'm here, sweetie. I'm right here."

Peg gave her mom a wan smile and grabbed Marge's wrist as a pain came. She squeezed so tightly she left indentations as her grip subsided and the worst of the pain passed. "I love you, Mom," she whispered.

Marge stroked Peg's forehead. "Oh, honey, I love you, too!"

Within the hour, Peg was back in her room. She had a new son named Daniel in the nursery. Pleasantly exhausted, Peg drifted off to sleep, and Marge went home to Jim and her other two children.

Coping with After-Baby Blues

Later that day, when Peg awoke, she was dismayed to find that the effects of *body-shock* had set in. She was stiff and sore. Her muscles ached. She was having afterbirth pains as her uterus began contracting back to normal size. Her vaginal area, especially where she'd been stitched, felt seared.

A nurse came in to have her get up to go to the bathroom, and Peg could hardly manage it. As Peg stood under a warm stream of water in the shower a short while later, she was very disappointed to see the *pouchiness* of her stomach. She had envisioned her flat, teenage stomach reappearing immediately.

Two days later, Peg was anxious to take Daniel home. However, she was completely shocked to find herself weak, worn-out, and feeling blue by the end of the first day out of the hospital. She just had not anticipated the amount of difficulty involved in birthing a child and recovering.

Home was with her parents, sister and brother. Peg and Daniel had a room to themselves near Marge and Jim's. After arriving late in the morning, Peg had put Daniel's few clothes in one drawer of their dresser, tucked him into his wicker basket, and prepared eight bottles with formula and sterilized nipples for the first 24 hours on their own. As she sat at the kitchen table watching two squirrels playing in the trees outside, Peg felt depressed.

When Marge returned home from the supermarket, she found Peg still sitting there, tears streaming down her face. "Oh, Peg," she said, "whatever is the matter?"

"I don't know, Mom," Peg gulped. "I thought this would be such a happy day! And here I am, all depressed and scared."

"What are you scared about, honey?"

"I don't know—that I can't take good care of Daniel, I guess. And you and Dad have to help me so much! And I've put you through all this!"

Marge sat down near her daughter and said gently, "Peg, you know, this is a natural thing to go through for any new mother at any age. They sometimes call it the *after-baby blues.*

"You get home and, all of a sudden, the responsibility is yours. The nurses aren't there to help when the baby cries. You can't send him back to the nursery when you're tired. And the rest of us are going about our usual routine.

"Yet, you don't have a usual routine. You are in the process of making up a new one, which will include another person from now on. You don't know how it will go, so you're scared. That's to be expected.

"Also, your hormones are playing tricks on you for now, Peg. The levels of your estrogen and progesterone are adjusting after the birth. Believe me, you'll be fine. You'll feel much better as each day passes.

"There will be some rough moments ahead, getting used to all this, but we're here. We'll stick with you, and you mustn't ever think you're a burden! The Lord has trusted us to help you, and we're grateful for His trust. We'll take one day at a time and solve problems as they come, not worry about them beforehand."

Adjusting to the New Baby

The next several days went more smoothly. Peg's depression lessened, she felt physically better, and got her rosy color back.

It was the night that brought problems now. Daniel was colicky, and seemed to have his days and nights confused. He slept contentedly most of the daytime hours, and then woke fitfully every two or three hours throughout the night.

As the weeks wore on, however, Daniel settled nicely into a routine. He was a healthy, adorable baby, and filling his needs as a family drew Peg, her parents, and her siblings closer together, as no other team experience had before. They delighted in Daniel, laughed and cried over him, and enjoyed their time together in many new ways. Of course, all days were not easy. Not all days ever are, but this family's attitude was one of acceptance, gratitude, and unity. The Lord called upon them, and they rose in the Spirit to meet His call.

With a teenage parent, there are certainly numerous special needs and concerns. However, people are people. With healthy attitudes and approaches, the Lord will bless your efforts. Proverbs 16:3 says: *Commit to the Lord whatever you do, and your plans will succeed.*

With teen parents, there are unique pitfalls to try and avoid—different ones for single parents than for marrieds—and both of these will be discussed in the next two chapters.

S.O.S. #13

1. **Have you explored the educational alternatives in your area for your pregnant teenager?**
2. **Have you considered what you might contribute to her ongoing life education?**

What Can You Do?

1. Contact any/all of the following resources with questions about your teen's education: the local high school or administrative offices of your school district; member(s) of your school board; any local vocational/technical school, junior or city college or university in

your area; an individual educator with whom you are acquainted or one to whom you are referred; a guidance or career counselor; and/or the Social Services Department in your county.

2. Contact your local Mental Health Facility. Inquire about the availability of any support groups that might be active in your area (and possibly of tremendous use to your teen in her learning, growth, and connections with others). For example, a local hospital might offer prenatal parenting classes. If there are elements of alcohol or drug abuse involved in your teen's pregnancy, groups such as Al-Anon or Al-Ateen may greatly benefit her.

   There are many other national associations, which might have local chapters. These can be most helpful, and their services are often provided free of charge or for a nominal fee.

3. Assess your teen's daily environment. If she lacks the company of others, is depressed or resentful, has been suffering an extreme erosion of her self-esteem, or is exhibiting signs that she is giving in to hopelessness, talk to her or a professional caregiver about ways to creatively correct the unhealthy direction her life education is taking her.

4. Have the teen list her general and specific life interests, such as sports, the sciences, writing, working with children, cooking, etc. Help her to sift through these interests to establish and begin achieving goals for herself, both personally and professionally, by channeling her energies. For instance, you might buy your teen books on catering as a business that would aid her in turning her cooking skills into a self-supporting enterprise. Likewise, literature on careers in the sciences might provide the impetus for her to

seek out the educational means to become a laboratory technician.

S.O.S. #14

Are you experiencing problems that stem from having a pregnant teenager in your life?

What Can You Do?

1. Know that resentment, repulsion, and frustration are powerful feelings. It is essential that you accept the fact that you are not a bad person for having any or all of these feelings. You cannot prevent feelings—they merely exist. What is important is that you try to restrain yourself from acting out your feelings by harming yourself or someone else. Rather, attempt to find a healthy outlet for these emotions. Some may be: (1) talking to a trusted friend, relative or professional; (2) listing on paper the feelings you have toward those involved. This list is for your eyes only—when you have written them down, you have taken a great step toward literally *getting them out of your system,* and you should then rip the paper into tiny pieces and throw it away; (3) In private, say your feelings aloud, as if you were actually speaking to your teen—this can also ease the emotional tension within yourself and put it into perspective; (4) cry; (5) pound a pillow; (6) get a good Christian book on handling negative emotions.
2. Many present problem areas of your life have roots in old life influences (*cobwebs,* if you will). It does not necessarily take years in analysis to identify what

very well may be irrelevant, obsolete limitations in the present. Two large keys to shedding unnecessary and ineffective feelings can be found in Ephesians 4:22-24: *You were taught, with regard to your former way of life, to put off your old self, which is being corrupted by its deceitful desires; to be made new in the attitude of your minds; and to put on the new self, created to be like God in true righteousness and holiness.*

The keys here are the words *deceitful* and *attitude.* Deceitful indicates that your *old self* may be falsely directing your current desires (and feelings). This Scripture specifically says that a new attitude in the mind is a prerequisite to being like God.

In order to put off your former self, you must first recognize what areas of your current attitude are deceitful, misleading you. Is it possible that resentment toward your pregnant teen comes from an old resentment of your own mother when she was pregnant with a younger sibling? Could you be repulsed at the sight of your daughter's pregnancy because your own father seemed repulsed toward women who were pregnant, or made derogatory remarks about them? Does your extreme frustration stem from your lack of control over the situation, which, in turn, reminds you of this same frustration over the demands placed on you to fill your family's needs?

Once you have recognized what a particular cobweb is, you can concentrate on changing your attitude. To do this, you must turn to the heavenly Father through Christ. Read 2 Corinthians 5:17-21, which indicates that we should reconcile ourselves to God through Christ. This is possible by an incredibly direct avenue: faith! Romans 5:1 says: *Therefore, since we have been justified through faith, we have peace with God through our Lord Jesus Christ.*

Faith is an active process of believing. First Thessalonians 1:3 tells us: *We continually remember before our God and Father your work produced by faith, your labor prompted by love, and your endurance inspired by hope in our Lord Jesus Christ.*

Therefore, to begin to change negative feelings and attitudes and to accept them during the process of this change, you must actively believe that God will make you new as you place your faith in Jesus, knowing He can truly heal your old hurts, dispel old notions, and help you reconcile your feelings to your pregnant teen, much as God reconciled us to Him through Jesus.

3. Be assured that not only are the Father and Son with you, but the Holy Spirit lives with you, also. When the directions by which you are to live seem too many and threaten to overwhelm you, refer to John 14:26,27. Jesus says here: *But the Counselor, the Holy Spirit, whom the Father will send in my name, will teach you all things and will remind you of everything I have said to you. Peace I leave with you; my peace I give you. I do not give to you as the world gives. Do not let your hearts be troubled and do not be afraid.*
4. Sort through each of the problems you are having with your pregnant teen or spouse and honestly question your reactions. If you find you are running on automatic pilot, interacting with responses that are not necessary or pertinent, make every effort to change your responses.

List under separate columns on paper: (1) what the problem area is; (2) how you are reacting to it; (3) the reasons why; and (4) how you might react more positively.

If you are still having trouble dealing with any of the problems, take another sheet of paper and list under new columns: (1) the problem; (2) the advantages and disadvantages of staying the same; and (3) the drawbacks and benefits of change. Discuss these with your teen, spouse, a friend, or a professional care-giver.

5. Get good Christian books on communication, intimacy, working out emotional conflicts, and practice the principles of positive, healthy interaction with those with whom you are having trouble dealing.

Our Hand in His

1. Have you provided for the continuing education of your pregnant teen, keeping the following reasons in mind: (a) continuity in her life; (b) contact with other people; and (c) ongoing learning/life education?
2. Are you taking the responsibility that Christians have to inspire and strengthen each other seriously? First Thessalonians 5:11 says: *Therefore encourage one another and build each other up.*
3. Are you helping your teen establish and work toward achieving goals? Proverbs 13:12 tells us the importance of hope and fulfillment of goals in our lives: *Hope deferred makes the heart sick, but a longing fulfilled is a tree of life.*
4. Have you found a way to accept and/or change any feelings of repulsion, resentment, anger, and/or frustration toward your pregnant teen?
5. Have you cleaned out the cobwebs of any past influences that may be affecting your feelings toward your teen? Turn to Hebrews 4:12-16, that you might be reminded of God's omnipotent knowledge of our

hearts and minds; also, that you might confidently confess your negative attitudes and receive His mercy, grace, and help in putting on a new self!

6. Have you genuinely communicated together, sorting through the various subconscious mind-tapes that might be playing while you react to them automatically? With your spouse, teen, or some other person, sort through any unwarranted messages to which you may be reacting.
7. Are you working earnestly toward eliminating any reactions you are having that are obsolete?
8. Have you established a sound physical and mental care program with your pregnant teen?
9. Do you recognize the magnitude of effects a pregnancy has on the development of a growing mind and body? Can you help your teen prepare for/overcome any of the effects that might be negative?
10. Have you been considerate of a pregnant teen's seeming preoccupation with such things as stretch marks?
11. Have you checked with your group or private health insurance to see if your pregnant teen's medical care costs or those of a newborn infant will be covered? How about the father's family's insurance program(s)?
12. If there is no insurance coverage that can pay the costs, have you made prior arrangements with the doctor(s) or hospital regarding payments?
13. If you cannot afford any of the above, have you contacted an attorney, doctor, church, state, or local Social Service Agency to inquire about any indigent aid programs that might be available to you?
14. Have you inquired with the doctor and hospital about how they handle complications and emergency care for mother and/or child in regard to who is able to pay what, and when? For instance, will they perform ser-

vices, transfer your teen and/or her child?

15. If you are very upset and worried over the financial obligations of the pregnancy, birth, and postpartum care, have you considered the wisdom of what Jesus tells us in Luke 12:27-31? *Consider how the lilies grow. They do not labor or spin. Yet I tell you, not even Solomon in all his splendor was dressed like one of these. If that is how God clothes the grass of the field, which is here today, and tomorrow is thrown into the fire, how much more will he clothe you, O you of little faith! And do not set your heart on what you will eat or drink; do not worry about it. For the pagan world runs after all such things, and your Father knows that you need them. But seek his kingdom, and these things will be given to you as well.*
16. Have you creatively planned for balancing financial, physical, and mental needs with your teen?
17. Are you letting pride get in the way of seeking necessary financial aid? Proverbs 29:23 says: *A man's pride brings him low, but a man of lowly spirit gains honor.*
18. Is the issue of money in a Christian perspective in your life? Hebrews 13:5 clearly directs us: *Keep your lives free from the love of money and be content with what you have, because God has said, "Never will I leave you; never will I forsake you."*
19. Have you calmly discussed the process of labor and childbirth with your teen?
20. Does she have fears that you might help her put to rest? Or can you refer her to dependable reading or to her doctor in order to aid her in overcoming/tolerating any anxiety?
21. Have you prepared yourself to remain a calm, strengthening presence during your teen's labor and/or the childbirth?

22. Have you discussed with your teen that the bonding process between her and her newborn is not necessarily an immediate, overwhelming attachment? Have you explained that real bonding happens over a period of time?
23. Have you also talked about after the baby is born—the period that often brings with it a time of depression, feeling frightened and/or lonely, questioning one's ability to fulfill the great responsibility of parenting?
24. Have you let your teen know that she is not a burden to you? Have you considered the great trust the Lord has placed in you to help her and her infant make their way in life?
25. Have you considered that, in the less than ideal circumstances of teenage parenthood, comes the opportunity to grow within the Body of Christ? Ephesians 4:16 says: *From him the whole body, joined and held together by every supporting ligament, grows and builds itself up in love, as each part does its work.*

CHAPTER FIVE

Looking Ahead to the Pitfalls

Amanda!" Carol Miller called to her 17-year-old daughter. "Amanda! Hurry up! You're going to be late!"

"Okay, okay." Amanda came rushing from her room. "I'm hurrying, Mom!"

Hopping on one foot while pulling a sock onto the other, Amanda's long brown curls bounced around her pretty face. Carol smiled at the comical scene. "I know you are, Amanda. It's just that the first impression you make at a new job is so important, and I don't want you to make a bad one."

"I won't, Mom." Amanda stood up from tying her shoes. "I just had to tuck Steve in after his bath."

FINDING A JOB AND DAY CARE

Steve, Amanda's four-month-old son, was going to stay with Carol two of the five days a week that Amanda would work as a receptionist for an automobile manufacturer. The other three days Amanda would take him to a neighborhood woman with a day-care home.

Today, Carol reflected back over the last year of the Miller family's life. They had gone over and over every detail among themselves during the months of Amanda's pregnancy in order to make all the decisions necessary for her to begin the process of piecing together a new lifestyle for herself. Knowing almost from the beginning that Amanda would keep her baby had allowed them the time needed to really address all of the issues involved.

Financially, it was impossible for Carol and her husband, Dave, to carry the load while Amanda continued to attend regular high school classes and retain the freedom of not working.

Neither could they afford separate housing arrangements for Amanda and her child, so it was quickly decided that Amanda and the baby would live with Dave, Carol, and Amanda's younger brother, Kent. Amanda had a large bedroom. By carefully arranging the furniture and putting up a decorative folding screen, the room was divided so the baby could have his own nook and Amanda could keep her privacy.

Carol, working three days a week as a Special Education teacher, was prepared to help care for Amanda's baby on her days off when Amanda found employment. It was decided Amanda would continue attending regular high school classes until the ninth month of her pregnancy. Then she would be at home until her baby was eight weeks old. Barring any unforeseen problems, and being able to use this period for planning and preparation, Amanda would begin to seek out employment during this time.

Amanda had been an average student in nearly all of her school subjects. Her personality strengths were most obvious in her friendliness, ability to get along well with others, pleasant disposition, and aptitude for organization.

The specific job skill that Amanda possessed was typing. She had been interested in the public relations field as a career possibility for some time. Bearing this in mind, Dave and Carol encouraged Amanda to think about taking a step toward this end by searching for a receptionist's position. This seemed the best choice since Dave and Carol were very concerned that Amanda not entangle herself in a career channel that was not easily expanded upon or changed as she matured into a woman.

Amanda felt at the time that Dave and Carol were being picky, but Dave assured her it was very important that they pay attention to details.

Carol had said, "It is essential that we think ahead, Amanda. Whether you find public relations is the career for you, or if you decide it's not, you will be able to apply the people-skills you learn as a receptionist to your career goals all across the board. Planning steps one at a time can save years of frustration and unhappiness later on in your life."

Dave agreed. "The point, Amanda, is that what you do now can be the all-important cornerstone in the foundation of a successful career that you love 20 or 30 years from now."

"Gee," Amanda had answered, "you guys make it sound like I have one shot at a career and that's it!"

"We don't mean to be overly cautious, Amanda," Carol said, "but we have seen the problems that people have had to deal with because of poor choices. And we want to help you make the best out of the difficult situation you're already in. Certainly, something like a job choice is not irreversible, and any experience can enhance your character—good or bad. Whatever we live through can make us better people."

"Especially if we trust our lives to the Lord," Dave put

in. "You know what Jesus says in Mark 11:22 and 23, Amanda: *Have faith in God . . . . I tell you the truth, if anyone says to this mountain, 'Go, throw yourself into the sea,' and does not doubt in his heart but believes that what he says will happen, it will be done for him.* We have a long road ahead of us, but we know that all will be well if we do our best and believe that the Lord will guide us."

With Amanda going to work full time, and the family's schedule already being extremely full, the three decided that Amanda would finish high school by using a series of home-study materials, and then take an exam that was available at a nearby city college.

Amanda opted to pace her studies over a year's time and take her exam then. A certified copy of proof that she was actively enrolled in these studies and would receive her general education diploma from the State Department of Public Instruction when she passed the exam was acceptable in order to validate that Amanda was qualified for the various jobs for which she interviewed several weeks later.

LIVING ON A BUDGET

In the meantime, Dave, Carol, and Amanda also developed a projected budget of income and expenses, which Amanda could realistically deal with while, at the same time, saving enough money to become self-supporting within two or three years after her baby was born.

They figured that Amanda would probably gross approximately $200 a week. Subtracting an (amply) estimated $160 for taxes, car expenses (Carol and Dave gave Amanda a dependable used car as a gift), lunches, clothing, day care, personal items for Amanda, and necessities for the baby, they then planned that the young girl would continue the family tradition of giving 10 percent of her income to their church and put 10 percent into a savings account. Her income now balanced out evenly with her expenses. This certainly did not allow for any frills, and it was accomplished with Carol and Dave footing the bill for Amanda and the baby's food and shelter. But, under the circumstances, it would be sufficient and would allow for some adjustments.

Most importantly, financially, it would initiate sound habits of budgeting, self-discipline, and money management, which could last Amanda a lifetime.

In a year, she would have more than $1,000 in her savings account. Hopefully, her job would provide health insurance (if not, Dave and Carol were prepared to keep Amanda on, and add the baby to, their group policy through Dave's company). Additionally, of course, it was hoped that Amanda's income would increase over a period of time. If she could save the money for necessary furnishings over a couple of years, handle her finances very carefully, and increase her income 5-10 percent each year, then Amanda could meet her goal, which was to live independently by her twentieth birthday.

MAKING TIME FOR PERSONAL NEEDS

The next subjects discussed involved Amanda's personal needs. Reasonably, they knew that a teenage girl could not keep up the full load of job, baby, and studies without setting aside some time for herself. Therefore, the three agreed to set aside two evenings a week for Amanda to socialize. One she would use to help out the youth group at church; the other at her own discretion. Dave and Carol would care for the baby these evenings.

On Saturdays, Amanda was in charge of cleaning the

family home and supervising her brother, Kent, with his share of the chores.

On Sundays, Amanda would help in the nursery at church during one service, then leave the baby in the nursery while she attended the other service.

FRAYED NERVES AND MOUNTING TENSIONS

It had taken Amanda two months to find a receptionist's position that was suitable. "Mom!" Amanda's exclamation broke into Carol's reverie. "Where are you?! I said goodbye three times!"

"I'm sorry, Amanda," Carol said. "I was just thinking about all that we've been through this last year, and now, here you are ready to go off on the first day of your new job!"

"Yep." Amanda's blue eyes twinkled. "And I really am going to be late if I don't get going. See ya tonight!"

"Good luck!" Carol waved her daughter off into the real world of a single working mother—a child in a grown-up's role.

In the weeks that followed, reality held some very harsh lessons for young Amanda. The daily routine's newness soon wore off. Getting up at five o'clock in the morning, showering, dressing herself, then feeding, bathing and dressing Steve, eating her own breakfast, and leaving the house by seven o'clock in order to drop Steve off at the sitter's, driving 45 minutes on the freeway to work, parking the car, and being at her desk by eight usually left Amanda breathless.

The office was a fast-paced one. The days flew by. Amanda was tired when five o'clock came. Then she had to call up an extra reserve of energy to drive to the babysitter, pick up Steve, get him and all the normal baby paraphernalia into the car, then drive to the house, feed her baby his dinner almost immediately, help Carol prepare for the rest of the family's evening meal, eat her own dinner (hopefully Steve would be content in his infant seat at least part of this time), help clean up the dishes, get Steve ready for bed, give him a bottle, and rock him to sleep.

By eight-thirty in the evening, after an already full 15-hour day, Amanda was exhausted. Most evenings, she would get her study materials out and fall asleep trying to concentrate on them.

As the weeks turned into months and Steve became more active, the strain increased. Amanda's nerves grew frayed, and tensions mounted among all of the household members.

Amanda began to shirk many of her duties at home, then her studying, as well. Finally, she left Steve more and more to Carol's care by conveniently *remembering* important phone calls or appointments to keep.

Knowing that Amanda was struggling with many pressures, Dave and Carol tried to be tolerant. They let the situation go until it was starting to tell on them, too. They realized that, as a youngster herself, Amanda still needed their love and attention.

When things got to the point where the Millers were snapping at one another, followed by days of silence, they finally sought the help of their pastor. An understanding woman with her own family, Pastor Douglas had some helpful guidelines for Dave, Carol, and Amanda.

She spoke to the issue of their unanimous weariness first. "Galatians 6:9 tells us, *Let us not become weary in doing good, for at the proper time we will reap a harvest if we do not give up*. Now, I know that sounds very burdensome and idealistic at the moment, but let's examine the dynamics of what's going on here. I do not doubt that each one of you has legitimate complaints and concerns about the conditions under which you are living. It is obvious that the level of stress is tremendous and you need some guidance in relieving or, at least, balancing it.

Inwardly, they were afraid that they were not in positions to risk exposing some of the resentments, concerns, and frustrations that were uncovered during counseling.

"Knowing how carefully you have all planned for the orchestrating of Amanda's pregnancy and keeping her baby, it doesn't surprise me that you are disconcerted over the impasse you seem to have reached. You're naturally feeling exhausted from bearing up for so long. Now, it's time to sort through the sources of stress in your master plan, explore what's working and what's not, and see what adjustments we can make."

FINDING SOLUTIONS

Dave, Carol, and Amanda counseled with Pastor Douglas for eight weeks. During this time, the family came to view their full, frantic schedules as a subconscious *running away* from each other; if their daily lives were so busy that there wasn't really time to be together, then they didn't have to face one another. Inwardly, they were afraid that they were not in positions to risk exposing some of the resentments, concerns, and frustrations that were uncovered during counseling. In their minds, the three had silently agreed, without consciously knowing it, to keep these negative emotions inside and not make waves in their home life. In their eyes, this would enable them to survive the pressure-packed circumstances.

Each week, Pastor Douglas gently brought them back to the verse she had first quoted from Galatians. She reminded them that, when they feel too weary to carry on, they should try to think of Steve and what a worthwhile effort it was working toward his well-being. She also pointed out that the harvest of his growing into a well-adjusted, loving adult would be one reward at the proper time for their not having given in to their exhaustion and problems now.

Specifically, Pastor Douglas strongly recommended cutting loose some of the structure in Amanda's life. The young woman was trying to deal with overwhelming guilt, self- and parental-imposed expectations, and striving to become a good mother. Her days were so demanding that her feelings were being stuffed, one after the other, inside herself, piling up to the point of nearly toppling her over emotionally. Pastor Douglas suggested that Amanda stop helping with the youth group at church and the nursery on Sundays. This brought an aggravated response from Carol.

"These are important obligations for Amanda to fulfill, Pastor! She shouldn't give them up."

"To whom are they important, Carol? To Amanda, or to you? Please think about this. I know that you have Amanda's very best interests at heart but, within all of our personal relationships, we must sometimes ask ourselves to starkly examine some of our own motives."

In the end, Carol realized that it was important to her that their church family visibly see the good things that Amanda did so they would supposedly think well of the girl, despite her having an out-of-wedlock child. Carol was able to admit that Amanda's welfare was more imperative than what others might think, and she recognized that Amanda's value to God was not based on how good she was or what she did. God loved Amanda as she was. When Carol saw how cleverly ulterior motives can disguise themselves as self-justified righteousness, she began to explore deeply all aspects of her relationship with Amanda, Dave, Kent, Steve, and herself. Dave was so moved by the courage and success of Carol's voluntary journey into her emotions that he initiated a search into his own feelings and ideas. This helped smooth the family's relationships quickly and successfully.

In addition to stopping her volunteer work at church, Amanda also put aside her studies for her high school proficiency exam for two or three years, when Steve would be older. Her employer knew her well enough by now to agree that this would not jeopardize her position with the company. In fact, he was so impressed by Amanda's gumption and perseverance in her efforts to hold down a job and be a caring mother to her son, all the while growing into an adult herself, he asked Amanda if she would like to participate on a committee to develop a day-care facility on-site for children of company employees. Amanda was flattered to accept, and ecstatic six months later to take a position as the day-care center's assistant director, complete with a $50-a-month raise.

This greatly eased the tension at home for Carol, as Steve was now at the day-care center all five days a week. By this time, Steve was 16 months old and a very active toddler. This was causing irritation in the evenings as Dave tried to relax from a hard day's work, and 12-year-old Kent's play was often interrupted by Steve's antics.

Dave and Carol decided to approach Amanda about an adjusted living arrangement. With Dave's being in the building business and Amanda now having nearly $1,100 in her savings account, they proposed a studio apartment-type addition to the back of their home, which would include a bathroom and kitchenette. Though Amanda and Steve would be cramped, the plan was sufficient for the next several months. By purchasing secondhand furniture and appliances, Amanda could provide for herself. Dave and Carol would pay for the construction. When Amanda moved out in the future, the addition would be turned into a family and game room. Everyone greeted this proposition with excited anticipation.

There were various other rough areas that the Miller's met, dealt with and lived through. Happily, however, on Steve's third birthday (just after Amanda's twentieth), the family celebrated by moving the young mother and Steve into a two-bedroom apartment, 20 minutes from the Miller's home and 25 minutes from Amanda's work. Amanda hoped that if she worked very hard she might be the director of the day-care center some day. For now, she could get by on her own if she was extremely cautious about how she spent her money.

GOD'S PROMISE FOR THE FUTURE

When Amanda was 23, she married a nice man she had met through contacts at work. Over the years, the couple has struggled with many different family issues—blending a new marriage with parenthood is never easy. The couple had difficulty with topics such as disciplining Steve; time divisions between the marital relationship, parenting, and alone time; financial responsibilities; and setting other household priorities. Additionally, when Amanda gave birth to a second child, then a third, there were extensive periods of pressure and tension over Steve's position in the family. As he grew older, there were times of intense jealousy and rivalry among the siblings. In his early teens, Steve went through a phase of rebellion toward the father who had raised him, and manifested this by threatening to seek out his biological father. These are but a few of the deeply emotional subjects that families must face in the aftermath of teenage pregnancy and life restructuring. Helping a young woman through can be an extreme hardship for the closest of families. God's promise in Isaiah 41:10 assures us that He is never far away, helping to hold us up while we do what is good and right in our lives: *So do not fear, for I am with you; do not be dismayed, for I am your God. I will strengthen you and help you; I will uphold you with my righteous right hand.*

REBUILDING DAMAGED RELATIONSHIPS

After the birth of 16-year-old Tammy's baby daughter, Jayne, Tammy went through a period of extreme loneliness and depression. The teenager imagined herself doomed to a lifetime of diapers and parents' tyranny. Tammy's parents, Rose and Alan, were having particular difficulty accepting their daughter's single motherhood, and had announced an entire list of rules that Tammy would now be expected to live by. There were more curfews and restrictions for Tammy to obey now than before she got pregnant. Among them was that Tammy was only to socialize within the confines of supervised church gatherings. Rose insisted that if Tammy was ever to find a man to love her and take on the great responsibility of Jayne, she must publicly prove her *repentance* by leading a meticulously chaste life-style.

Alan and Rose were so overzealous in their efforts to reform and protect Tammy's reputation that they completely stifled any recuperation or growth of the girl's self-esteem. She began to see herself as completely unworthy, to the point that she could not foresee anyone loving her again, especially enough to be her mate. Tammy even thought that God had forsaken her, forgotten that she existed. This left her so desolate that she began contemplating suicide. However, her innate sense of survival and buoyant teenage attitude soon had her channeling her emotions into anger at her parents.

She used the only defense she felt she had available—Jayne. Tammy began to manipulate her parents by either offering them access to Jayne or keeping them from her altogether. Rose and Alan soon caught on to this game plan of Tammy's and were infuriated by her obvious attempt to manipulate them. They, in an ill-devised attempt to correct her, pounced on her in her bedroom one evening.

They ranted and raved about how childish and selfish she was acting, and told her that, if she didn't straighten up right away, they would cut off the financial help they were giving her.

Tammy, terrified, and feeling she was totally at her parents' mercy, shouted a stream of insults and threats of her own. The confrontation was interrupted only when Jayne's cries caught their attention. Rose and Alan steamed off to another part of the house, while Tammy tended to Jayne.

The next day, Rose and Alan presented Tammy with the news that they were taking her to their pastor's office so that she could be counseled on the way a proper Christian girl should act.

Pastor Yates requested that Rose and Alan remain at his first few sessions with Tammy. Knowing the family somewhat, the pastor suspected that the parents, as much as Tammy, had a need for guidance in their perspective of the situation.

It became immediately apparent that he was correct. Rose and Alan took turns self-righteously quoting Bible verses totally out of context, until Pastor Yates could remain silent no longer.

"May I suggest we start our work here with a particular Scripture?" he asked.

"Of course," Rose answered, smiling smugly at Alan. "That's why we're here—so that you can make Tammy see what she won't learn from us!"

Pastor Yates thought that Rose reminded him a little of a hen strutting her seniority around the barnyard. "Yes, well," he said, clearing his throat, "the verse I had in mind applies to the two of you as much as to Tammy. Romans 8:1 and 2 say: *Therefore, there is now no condemnation for those who are in Christ Jesus, because through Christ Jesus the law of the Spirit of life set me free from the law of sin and death.*"

After many weeks, Rose and Alan came to see that the humble, gentle love of Jesus does not delight in self-serving dominance or judgment. Rather, His desire is that we recognize our equal value in God's eyes, as well as our equal capacity for sin. Pastor Yates emphasized the stories in John 8:1-7 and Luke 7:36-48.

He also helped Tammy to see that she was being unfair with her parents, Jayne, and herself. He pointed out that she was wrong to use her child to hurt her parents. He impressed upon her that she was a lovable, good person, with her whole life ahead of her.

With the pastor's help, Rose, Alan, and Tammy developed a policy of mutual consideration to start over in their efforts to live at peace with one another. Their main points of concern were as follows:

1. They would go slowly—not push so hard for conformation on any of their parts.

2. They would strive to treat one another with respect.

3. They would try very hard to accept their differences and their right to separate opinions as the individuals they were.

Healthy relationships take time to form, and when there has been a breach, healing must be allowed to take place.

---

4. They would try to listen to one another's feelings closely.

5. They would not express their anger toward one another by name-calling or overbearing threats.

6. They would attempt to express their love for one another through actions and gestures in order to nurture their family along toward contentment and happiness.

Pastor Yates encouraged the family to be patient and pray for God's help. He noted that healthy relationships take time to form, and when there has been a breach, healing must be allowed to take place.

DATING AGAIN

Kate Simpson, 15, sat at the kitchen table, nervously strumming her fingers on its surface. She was going on her first date since the birth of her baby daughter three months before. Kate had mentally gone over and over what dating again might be like. In the small rural town where she lived, it would be difficult to live down the reputation of being a single, teenage parent, even more so because the baby's father, Tyler, was to be an active presence in his daughter's life and made no secret of not having wanted to marry Kate. This caused an extremely deep wound in Kate, which made her very insecure about dating at all.

Kate's parents, Joe and Vivian, were no less nervous than Kate. They sat in the nearby living room, watching television without really seeing it. Their anxieties about Kate going out again were certainly understandable. Yet, they knew it was one more part of the whole process of Kate's growing up that they must get through as best they could. They had already talked extensively with her about beginning this phase of life over again.

There were three major areas of concern that Vivian had tried to underscore:

1. Because Kate had been sexually active before did not mean she need be so again, premaritally.
2. Kate was loved, supported, and needed by her family and friends; therefore, she could lean on them for any strength she might need along the way in redirecting her adolescent development.
3. Regardless of what was done, Kate's future was bright with opportunities.

Joe had given Kate a special greeting card just days before this night of her first date after becoming a parent. In it, he had simply written: "Philippians 3:13,14: *One thing I do: Forgetting what is behind and straining toward what is ahead, I press on toward the goal to win the prize for which God has called me.* All my love, Dad"

As you relate to your teen in the re-establishment

of her life's direction, make every effort to remember that it is never too late to begin anything or to start over in her daily life or with God. He is always waiting with His grace, love, and forgiveness!

BREAKING DESTRUCTIVE PATTERNS

Sadly, there are situations where, regardless of the well-intentioned attempts of loved ones to help a teenage parent in need, she doesn't rebound. There are a multitude of reasons for this, as well as situations where there just doesn't seem to be a reason.

Corinne's was one such case. She got pregnant at 14, gave her baby up for adoption, and was pregnant again by a different boy before her sixteenth birthday. This time, her parents reluctantly consented to marriage. Some months later, after her wedding and the birth of her son, she celebrated her seventeenth birthday by announcing over cake and ice cream at her parents' home that she and her infant son would be moving back in with them because she was getting a divorce and had nowhere else to go. Naturally disturbed but feeling as if they had no choice, Corinne's parents accepted her back home with their grandchild. They tried to help her in very giving and logical ways—with money, child care, emotional support, and love. But, to their complete astonishment and dismay, Corinne informed them shortly after her eighteenth birthday that she was pregnant again and wanted to borrow money from them for an abortion. They refused. Then they talked her into giving up this child, her third in six years, for adoption, also. The day Corinne came home from the hospital, her parents contacted a psychiatrist, referred to them by a friend, and made an appointment with him for their daughter.

After several consultations, Corinne summoned the courage to explain to her parents that her specific pattern of sexual behavior and pregnancy seemed to stem from several deep-seated emotional problems that caused her, much like someone who attempts suicide in succession, to cry for help by becoming pregnant. In this way, there was no denying Corinne attention. Fortunately, her repetitive cries were finally heard and her destructive pattern of behavior stopped. Corinne remained in treatment with her psychiatrist for two years. Her emotional problems were mostly solved, and the scars from her experience were minimized when, thankfully, she received Jesus Christ as Lord during this time period.

Starting over for a teen, after becoming a parent, can be lonely, confusing, frustrating, and frightening. Speaking to issues such as those that have been discussed here is not necessarily easy, but is a prerequisite to the teen's maturation into a stable, fully functioning adult. Through prayer, understanding, and loving actions, this emotional labyrinth can be traversed successfully.

FINANCIAL NEEDS

In the midst of such a turbulent experience as a teen pregnancy, families can be so distracted that they lose sight of the fact that there *is* a future. Your teen daughter *will* get to be 20 and 30. She *will* develop into an adult woman. With this in mind, there are certainly pitfalls to try to avoid, as well as some important steps that can be taken to help lay a healthy foundation on which she can build as her life unfolds.

One issue that is often overlooked, other than meeting

its immediate demands, is money. Of course, careful planning can make all the difference in a person's financial future. Rather than suffocating personal relationships and goals with money problems, some sound financial practices can be put into play, which will free everyone involved to build relationships and goals. There are three facts regarding money, which must be faced: (1) it takes money to live; (2) to get money, one must normally earn it; and (3) to have enough to live without undue pressures, there must be a healthy balance between giving, saving, and spending. This is not to say that money for luxuries will not be a problem for a long time, but actual financial needs for survival can be met with as little money pressure as possible.

An essential aspect to examine in regard to money is what the heavenly Father's involvement is. People often try to separate God from money as if He were in charge of our physical, mental, spiritual, emotional, and sexual well-being, but not our material condition. This is like saying that the trunk, branches, leaves, and bark of a tree have nothing to do with its fruit! God wants us to be happy. He wants us to feel fulfilled and secure. Like parents at Christmastime, God wants to give His children the best gifts. However, He also understands that, in the grand scheme of life, there are certain things that have to be taken care of before certain other things can come about. Take note of the physical and mental energy required during the child-rearing and career-building years of life. People could no more withstand the rigors of this time at age 10 than at 80! It is also highly possible that, until an adult has pulled his own weight, gained experience, and weathered several of life's storms, he is not ready to handle the responsibilities of too much financial freedom. God wants to be as sure as possible that His children have their priorities straight, that they can temper their use of money with the wisdom that comes during the seasoning of life. So, as a parent who refuses a five-year-old a chemistry set, God often expresses His love with a *wait-until-(or if) you-are-ready* answer to our wants. This means, then, that God will supply all of our material needs in the ways that are for our very best. If your teen is suffering from poor financial choices, which she has made, then it is safe to say that she definitely may need your experienced help in laying the groundwork for a healthy financial foundation for her future well-being.

ACHIEVING A HEALTHY SELF-ESTEEM

Following on the heels of money is the way to earn it, or the teen's career. One pitfall that a teenage parent can stumble into here is the smothering effects of futility. She may not be able to see that each step she takes does indeed contribute to a sound foundation for her future. An older, wiser adult may need to point this out. Approaching this subject with an attitude of helping the teen put as many of her interests and abilities to work for her as possible will hold her in good stead as these develop and others blossom in her personality. Today's society offers more opportunities than ever before for young women to try their hands individually at different career pursuits.

A hopeful veterinarian might work at a zoo or on a ranch in the beginning of her trek toward that end. A girl who would like to design fashion clothing may find that her interest wanes after working in a retail boutique. Yet another teen may feel so inspired by her employment at an interior decor supplier's that she takes evening classes until she earns a degree in interior design. Careers are like anything else—they are built upon the blocks of time, knowledge, and experience. There is hardly a greater inner confidence felt than that of a young mother who, entering her 20s, finds herself self-supporting because of her own hard work and creative effort. Self-confidence is a major ingredient in the mixture that also includes self-respect, self-motivation and self-awareness, together making up self-esteem.

Self-esteem—having a high regard and respect for self—necessarily must be connected with love. With a teen, care may need to be taken so that she does not confuse love of self with selfishness. Love, the most cherished aspect of the human condition, can also be the most misunderstood. Love, in its purest and most natural state, involves activity. You show you love yourself and others by the things you do and say. If you love yourself in a healthy way, you will eat, exercise, rest, dress, live, and interact with others in well-balanced, nurturing proportions. You will support yourself and those around you with loving actions.

As an essential member of the higher Body that is God's family, each person has an obligation to every other person. Romans 12, verses 4 and 5, tells us plainly, *Just as each of us has one body with many members, and these members do not all have the same function, so in Christ we who are many form one body, and each member belongs to all the others.* Therefore, it is essential that we treat ourselves and others as the privileged members of God's family that we all are. In this way, the foundation of life becomes stronger and more stable. This girds us up for the inevitable hardships that life brings. Your teenager will be exposed to hardships beyond her pregnancy just as surely as anyone else. No one escapes the opportunity to grow, or the challenge to realize the unique potential that God has placed within the fabric of every personality.

The foundation of a healthy life must include careful consideration for all of the elements mentioned here: money, planning, effort, career, self-esteem, love, and support of our fellowman. These combine to make your teen a ready canvas for the Creator's gentle hand.

There are special needs for teenage mothers, and avoiding the pitfalls awaiting them can require great finesse; but well-placed efforts are most certainly worth the benefits reaped!

S.O.S. #15

Are you trying to help your teen juggle the demands of school, job, baby, and self?

What Can You Do?

1. Recognize that your needs and circumstances are unique and that all of your plans, goals, and problem solutions should reflect this uniqueness.
2. Be prepared to make adjustments to your plans and goals all along the way. Don't be so inflexible that you miss opportunities to creatively relieve stress and tension.
3. Try to honestly examine your motives in regard to the help you are giving your teen in choosing directions. Be sure that you are not leading her for the fulfillment of your own purposes rather than hers. Read Proverbs 20:5, which says *The purposes of a man's heart are deep waters, but a man of understanding draws them out.*

4. Remember that your efforts are for the benefit of human lives. Consider how much energy you presently may put into your job, maintaining your home, or mastering a new leisure activity. Surely your daughter and grandchild are worth the greater amount of time, resources, and energy needed to help them realize a gratifying life.
5. Remember who you are really serving. Colossians 3:23,24 tells us distinctly: *Whatever you do, work at it with all your heart, as working for the Lord, not for men, since you know that you will receive an inheritance from the Lord as a reward. It is the Lord Christ you are serving.* By helping one another through the crisis of a teen pregnancy, you are, in fact, serving the Lord.

Our Hand in His

Considering the answers to the following questions may help you avoid some of the pitfalls that await unsuspecting teenage parents:

1. Have you seriously thought about the severe pressure a teenage mother may be under trying to juggle school, job, baby, and self?
2. Have you examined the situation closely and eliminated any unnecessary stress factors?
3. Are you prepared to put forth all the effort that will be required of you before your teen and her new baby can be ideally on their own?
4. Have you resolved that a natural part of your teen's redirecting her personal development will include dating?
5. Are you prepared to deal with this dating in a calm, encouraging manner?

6. Do you realize that preaching, threatening, and coercing are not what God wants you to do in guiding your teen onto a healthy life path?
7. Do you accept the fact that your teen is not one bit less of a person because of her pregnancy or having had a child of her own?
8. Do you have any reason to believe that your teen's pregnancy was actually a subconscious cry for help with deeper, inner troubles?
9. Have you addressed the issue of money in the laying of a healthy foundation for your teen's future?
10. Have you considered Luke 12:6,7? *Are not five sparrows sold for two pennies? Yet not one of them is forgotten by God. Indeed, the very hairs of your head are all numbered. Don't be afraid; you are worth more than many sparrows.*
11. Are you participating in aiding her to plan and pursue a career that will help her become self-supporting?
12. Is your teen's self-esteem suffering greatly? Or is she on the road to a wholesome recovery in regard to self and others?
13. Have you discussed with your teen that love is much more than the feelings of physical attraction and emotional warmth of a couple coming together?
14. Have you explained that love means doing loving things for self and others?
15. Have you made your teen aware that she is a vital member of God's family, the Body of Christ?
16. Are you prepared to be watchful for the many pitfalls that exist and can trap an inexperienced teenage mother in the areas of juggling her needs, dating, sex, money, career, self-esteem, love, and support of her fellowman?

CHAPTER SIX
Getting Married

Seventeen-year-old LuAnn, four months pregnant, and Corey, the father of her baby, were going to get married in eight weeks. There had been tremendous emotional turmoil in coming to this decision, but it was now made, and LuAnn's parents, Richard and Pat Roberts, were coming to accept that their daughter's marriage and parenthood were imminent. It was very difficult to envision their youngest child entering the adult world so abruptly; but, together with LuAnn and Corey and Corey's parents, Earl and Marion Howe, a wedding had been the agreed course of action. The date chosen was a few days after Corey's eighteenth birthday.

MAKING PLANS AND ARRANGEMENTS

Today, Pat and LuAnn would meet with the group of ladies at their church who would be serving lunch in the fellowship hall after the wedding ceremony. Pat had a sense of growing anxiety over having so many details to attend to in such a short period of time. There were invitations, flowers, photographer, cake, punch, the serving of lunch, the pastor, ceremony, music, dresses, two bridal showers, and related incidentals. As Pat was dressing to meet LuAnn at the church, the phone rang. It was Pat's mother. "Oh, Mom," Pat said, "I have to run. LuAnn and I have to be at the church in 20 minutes. I don't know if I'm going to make it through all of this or not!"

"Pat," the older woman responded, "slow down. Now that the decision is made, you need to enjoy! Don't look at LuAnn's wedding as a curse—give those kids the benefit of the doubt and have fun!"

"I'll try, Mom," Pat sighed. "Mostly, I just feel rushed."

The two said their good-byes, and Pat was off. The meeting went smoothly. LuAnn and Pat decided to go out for lunch afterward. They discussed who would be in the wedding party. LuAnn began excitedly ticking off the names of several high school friends that she and Corey were considering, but Pat interrupted. "Whoa, LuAnn! Stop a minute. Before you get too far into this, there's something you and Corey should think about. I know you are very close to your friends right now, but what about in five years? I'd hate for you to look at your wedding pictures, for example, and wish you'd had your brothers and sisters—you know they're forever—instead of school buddies you might grow away from."

LuAnn considered this point for a moment, "Hmm. Well, I suppose that is something we should talk about."

Mother and daughter moved on to plan in other areas. Every detail would pass by Corey and his mother before being finalized. Pat found herself having to slow LuAnn down in nearly every area of the wedding plans where expenses were concerned. LuAnn just had no concept of what things cost and how fast they added up.

As the pair reached the end of their lunch, Pat broached the subject of her thoughts on a wedding gift for the young couple. "You know, LuAnn, Dad and I have discussed two different options for our gift to you and Corey and we want your input about it. We wondered whether you'd rather have us buy you a washer and dryer, or pay for your honeymoon—"

"Eee!" LuAnn squealed. "No question—the honeymoon!"

"Hold up there, LuAnn." Pat raised a hand in midair. "This is something else you and Corey need to think about carefully. You know, the honeymoon won't last, but you'll be washing clothes for a long, long time. Laundromats can get pretty expensive and inconvenient."

"Okay, okay." LuAnn nodded. "I get the picture. Boy, Corey and I have a lot to talk over this week!"

TAKING TIME TO COUNT THE BLESSINGS

The next month passed by in a blur. As they attended to details and watched plans fall into place, Pat and Richard felt stress beginning to overcome them. There were house guests to prepare for, meals to ready and order, the rehearsal dinner to make reservations and menus for . . . . Pat's list of things to do seemed to keep growing longer. Fortunately, her mother was close by, and Richard's parents were coming in two weeks to help clean, plant flowers, and take care of last minute things that Richard and Pat would have no time for. There was to be a large gathering of their friends and relatives, as well as Corey's family, at the Roberts's home the evening of the wedding, so this made for even more work. At one point, Pat moaned to her sister on the phone, "This has gotten so far out of hand, I don't think I'll enjoy one minute of it!"

"Oh, Pat," her sister calmly replied, "weddings are stressful in the best of circumstances. You better get hold of yourself, or LuAnn's going to be gone, and you'll have missed the whole thing for worrying! Besides, you still

You need to learn how to be a marriage partner, just as you would learn to be a teacher or a lawyer.

have the weddings of two more kids to go, so look at this one as good practice. Everybody has to start somewhere!"

Pat took her sister's advice and tried to take time to experience the pleasures and excitement that the next weeks brought, instead of fretting needlessly over things that would simply work out one way or the other. Either way, the day would come, they would all do their best, and it would be over. One bright spot for Pat was the discovery that she and Richard genuinely enjoyed Corey's parents. Earl and Marion were nice people, easy-going, and more than willing to contribute their share to the wedding, both financially and time-wise. Pat decided that, given half a chance, there were plenty of blessings to count, even in this situation.

LAST-MINUTE PREPARATIONS

LuAnn and Corey attended weekly pre-nuptial counseling sessions with their pastor the last six weeks before their wedding. Pastor Marnell was a kindly, older gentleman who was very comfortable with the fact that God will turn hardship into blessing if only people will let Him. He addressed many issues in these few weeks, and was confident that LuAnn and Corey would seek his help if they needed it after their union when, as Pastor Marnell said, couples were often more ready to listen to someone outside of themselves. He said, ""If a time comes when you need my advice, some of what I've said now will filter back into your memory, and I hope that this will let you feel free to come here, or go to another reliable professional for help. Right now, you're naturally so excited that you can't possibly imagine anything tripping up the love you have for each other. But, you know, life can get to the best of us, and you need to learn how to be a marriage partner, just as you would learn to be a teacher or a lawyer. Of course, the difference is that you're married 24 hours a day, and it takes that much more energy to make a successful situation out of it. The most essential thing I can say to you is that you need the Lord. He's the only one who can turn toads into princes, and He'll do it, if you'll let Him."

LuAnn and Corey ran true to form and were so enamored of each other that they barely heard what Pastor Marnell told them, but the elder's words were tucked away into their minds to draw from later.

As the last two weeks before the wedding were upon them, Pat reflected on how supportive the parents of LuAnn's girlfriends had been. They had hosted a bridal shower and given the couple many beautiful gifts. They received very nice, practical things like towels, sheets, cookware, and small appliances that were necessary to run a household, yet expensive for a young couple to try to buy on their own. LuAnn delighted over these items, which it had not occurred to her to even think about. Bit by bit, the apartment LuAnn and Corey had rented a few miles from the Roberts's home was filled up. Corey's parents had given the couple a television for a wedding gift, and the youngsters had responsibly opted for the washer and dryer, rather than the honeymoon, from Pat and Richard. LuAnn had her own savings account that was to have been used for her miscellaneous expenses while in college, but she used this now to purchase good used furniture for their apartment, which she found by scouting sales and classified ads.

Two days before the wedding, Pat stood in the doorway of her daughter's bedroom as LuAnn finished packing her personal belongings into boxes to take to her new home. Pat thought she would never forget the mixture of hope and pain that pressed at her heart as her child carefully tucked the stuffed animals she'd had since she was a baby into a box to be saved for her own child's arrival in three short months.

THE ULTIMATE IN PLAYING HOUSE

The wedding went fine. LuAnn made a lovely bride and Corey, a handsome groom. There wasn't a dry eye in the church as the two were pronounced man and wife and left the church, looking not one day older than the teenagers they were. The pair went on a brief honeymoon to a city a few hours from home, and then they were back-to live, work, and play in the unfamiliar world of adulthood. The three months before their baby's birth were the last of the couple's free time. Corey went off to work in the mornings as a stock boy in a local grocery store, while LuAnn stayed at home to arrange and rearrange their new belongings. They often went out to fast-food restaurants or to a movie in the evenings. Money was extremely tight, but the young couple was otherwise content to cuddle on the sofa with television at night and visit family and friends on the weekends.

Pat, Richard, Earl, and Marion had all agreed to let their children be on their own unless they asked for help. A big bonus for the teenage couple was that, for the most part, they knew the basics necessary to keep their simple household functioning. Other than a few frantic calls about burned foods and lumpy mashed potatoes, the teens appeared to be doing well.

AND BABY MAKES THREE

One morning, Pat received a call at her office from Corey. "Pat? Guess what!" Corey sounded so excited he could hardly talk. "We just had a baby girl!"

"Oh, Corey!" Pat exclaimed. "Congratulations! Is she all right? Is LuAnn okay? How big is the baby?"

"Hold on," Corey interrupted her flow of questions. "LuAnn wants to talk."

"Mom," Luann's voice was weary, "we have a baby. She's perfect! We named her Nel."

Pat and Richard went to visit their new granddaughter at the hospital that night. LuAnn would be going home the next day because there was no insurance to pay the hospital or doctor bills. LuAnn would be home with the baby for six weeks and then would go out to work. However, the first two months with Nel were pretty rough. She fell prey almost immediately to some sort of respiratory infection and had to spend a night at the hospital in an oxygen tent. LuAnn and Corey were frightened and anxious over the tiny infant. When Nel came home, LuAnn was up with her most nights, holding her up to help ease the congestion in her chest. Pat spent three nights on the sofa in the couple's apartment so that LuAnn could get some much-needed rest. After the infection was gone, Nel was so used to her nightly rockings and being held that she insistently continued to cry until LuAnn gave in and picked her up. Corey needed his sleep to be able to work, so LuAnn withstood the lonely hours on her own.

As Nel's six-week checkup passed, so did the date for LuAnn to search for work. The young wife and mother assured her husband that she would go to work—soon.

REALITY BEGINS TO TAKE HOLD

Soon turned into weeks, then months. Corey could not withstand the pressures that were upon him any longer. He blew up at LuAnn. "You have to get a job! We're two months behind on the electric bill, I had to sell my guitar to pay the gas company, and everything's coming due again!"

Having been completely absorbed with filling Nel's needs, and using what little energy she had left to feel sorry for herself, LuAnn hadn't known there were serious problems with money. But she had noticed there wasn't any money left over for things like movies, clothes, or meals out. Under her own pressure and feeling very defensive, she screamed back at Corey, "Well, what do you expect? What would you like me to do—leave Nel on a curb, crying and sick, while I look for a job? Why don't you get more work? Or ask for a raise?"

Corey, already working between 40 and 50 hours each week, exploded in fury. "LuAnn, figure it out! I'm working as much as I can—it's just not enough! You have to help!"

LuAnn burst into tears and yelled, "Help? Help! What do you call cooking, cleaning, laundry, shopping, taking care of Nel, and keeping everything together here?"

"Together!" Corey was incredulous. "If you call this

whole deal *together,* I wonder what chaos is! We've got so many doctor bills piled up it'll take five years to pay them off; you've had a *headache* every night for three weeks, and I haven't had a clean shirt in two days!"

Corey and LuAnn argued heatedly back and forth for more than an hour. They released their frustrations in a destructive torrent of name-calling and sarcastic remarks. Nel was crying loudly in the background, and the small family ended their evening on an entirely miserable note.

GOING HOME TO MOTHER

The next several days were spent in cold silence. Inside, LuAnn and Corey felt sick and alone. They avoided each other long past the point when their anger had dissipated; but false pride took its place. Resentment and fear took root and began to grow. LuAnn started another argument one evening as Corey came home from work. Their words were loud and ugly as one attacked the other.

The fight ended with LuAnn grabbing Nel from her crib and storming off to her parents. When Pat opened the front door, LuAnn stood there with tears streaming down her face, holding Nel wrapped in a blanket. "Whatever is the matter?" Pat gasped.

As LuAnn sobbed out her story, Richard and Pat were sure of what to do. Richard drove to their apartment to bring Corey back. The four then sat up most of the night sorting through the young couple's problems.

"You must understand something, kids," Richard said. "Tempers are bound to flare up under pressure—for all marrieds, not just you. What you need to remember is that there are ways to fight fair. You have to learn these rules or you'll never grow beyond the emotional level you're at right now. The first rule is not to call names. I know you're under a lot of strain, and we'll see how Pat and I can help, but that can't be an excuse to verbally rip each other apart!"

After much discussion, it was decided that Corey would explain his financial situation to his boss and ask for a raise. If this was not forthcoming, Corey would look for another job. For the immediate future, Pat and Richard would advance LuAnn and Corey $500 to catch up on their bills. On Saturdays, the young parents would work off the loan while Nel stayed with the grandparents. One evening a week, Pat and Richard would also keep Nel so that the young couple could go for a ride, a walk, or to a movie. Richard went over the couple's income and expenses with them on paper and, together, they devised a reasonable budget. LuAnn did not feel that she had the stamina to work a full-time job, so Pat suggested she look for something a few evenings a week so Corey would have an opportunity to be alone with Nel. This would save them money they would ordinarily pay to sitters, allow LuAnn to continue as Nel's primary care-giver, and help Corey feel that he had some control over how his home was being run.

THE SITUATION WORSENS

Other ways of fighting fair were pointed out to Corey and LuAnn by the more experienced adults, such as confessing their anger to each other, redirecting their anger into other physical or mental activities, getting away from each other until they could calmly discuss their feelings, and being honest about what were legitimate feelings of anger toward each other and what were really inner fears and anxieties that the two actually shared but couldn't bring themselves to face.

These things all helped to take the pressure off temporarily but, after a few more months passed and reality for LuAnn and Corey stayed routine, as it does for most people, tension began building again. Corey began stopping off for a beer or two after work. LuAnn took this as a personal rejection of her and Nel. In order to get back at Corey, she started spending badly needed money on clothes, make-up, perfume, and jewelry. This totally exasperated Corey. He began staying away longer after work, warning LuAnn that she'd better not tattle to her parents again or she'd be sorry. Typically adolescent in their approach, these kinds of behavior become extremely dangerous in a teen marriage. Playing at being adults with no one to really stop them from harming themselves, LuAnn and Corey were involved in things that could be their demise, both as individuals and as a couple. Corey's leaning on alcohol could bring untold misery to all of their lives, and LuAnn's using money as a weapon could cripple them financially. By intimidating LuAnn into cutting off the comfort she took in being able to go to her parents, Corey was actually making an attempt—destructive though it might be—at exercising control over their lives.

After a few feeble efforts to communicate maturely and fight fair, the couple's adolescent natures took over completely and they were back at each other's throats with a fierceness that thoroughly belied their inner fears, disappointments, and resentments. A natural consequence of their behaviors left unchecked, the youngsters spiraled into hopeless depression. When LuAnn finally felt so helpless that she saw no hope of things ever setting themselves right, she packed her own and Nel's clothes one day and went to her parents. She told them her side of the marital problems with bitterness. It was all Pat could do not to take sides with her daughter. She saw LuAnn besieged by a thoughtless husband who was out among people all day—and now into the evenings—while his young wife was left alone to care for their home and child. But Pat kept her tongue, and wisely so. As Corey spilled his side in defense that evening, Pat saw that LuAnn was not really doing her part in the marriage, either. Calmly, so as not to encourage any hysterical, irrevocable action,

For this reason a man will leave his father and mother and be united to his wife, and they will become one flesh (Gen. 2:24).

Richard and Pat suggested that the couple seek help from Pastor Marnell.

HELPING WITH THE PIECES

Pastor Marnell was happy to have LuAnn and Corey in his counseling care. The first thing he suggested was that they try to pray together, asking that their hearts might be opened to each other. "You don't have to pray aloud if that makes you uncomfortable," the pastor said, "but hold hands for a few minutes and silently ask the Lord to help you begin to mend your relationship."

Next, the pastor directed Corey and LuAnn to 1 Corinthians 13. "This chapter tells us of the importance of love. It clearly describes that the greatest of all aspirations is to love and be loved. But it also plainly states what love is and is not. Read it together and, as you feel the pinch of recognizing what you are and are not doing to keep love in your hearts, pray that the Lord will enter your life in these areas so that you can begin to resolve your problems."

Pastor Marnell also explained the vital role of depending on each other for help in building up their marriage. "It's fine that you've gone to your parents for help, LuAnn, and that the two of you have now come to me. However, you must know and believe that there is not one other person who can make your marriage successful. You are both familiar with the Scripture, *For this reason a man will leave his father and mother and be united to his wife, and they will become one flesh* (Gen. 2:24). There is no other way to realize the kind of marriage God intends for you to have than to truly become one. Both man and woman should put away their dependence on parents, other relatives, and friends, and cleave to each other. The best we, who care for you, can do is to *love you alone.* You cannot get back the freedom that your teenage and single years were meant to hold for you. So, now, you must choose the direction that your lives will go in order to best combine your own growing-up with that of your child's. The success of this is largely determined by your attitudes toward yourselves and each other."

LuAnn and Corey were listening to Pastor Marnell closely this time, with a much different outlook from when they had sat before him a year earlier. They drank in his words with a desperate desire to find a way to make their marriage work. Their basic decency and respect for others, the goodness that marriage stood for in their eyes, and the preciousness of their daughter gave them the impetus to want to make their relationship last.

Pastor Marnell told them, "You mustn't let feelings of despair overwhelm you as you look to the difficulty of the task set before you. You can also take heart in the fact that, usually, when something is taken away from people, there is something else given in its place, or more bountifully bestowed in another area of your life. For instance, a blind person may not have his sight, but his other senses may become extremely heightened. You may not have the freedoms of youth, but you might find generous blessings in some other corner of your lives."

The couple saw Pastor Marnell twice a week for three months. On their last day, the kindly man sent them off with a Scripture. "In Matthew 19:14, Jesus said, *Let the little children come to me, and do not hinder them, for the kingdom of heaven belongs to such as these.* I sincerely hope you can bring yourselves to place your faith in the Lord, without doubt or fear, just as small children can do. Don't let the anxieties and roadblocks of this world stop you from achieving all the Lord has meant for you to be. I firmly believe your union can be renewed if you will try to look beyond the troubles of the moment, keep them in perspective, and enjoy the here and now."

A BRIGHTER TOMORROW

Teen pregnancy is not the condemnation of anyone's life. It is a consequence of some very poor choices on the part of two youngsters who are not in a position to be starting a family of their own. If anyone doubts the importance of life, family, and membership in the Body, one has only to look at the nature and longevity of this consequence. The Lord, in all of His wisdom, binds the teen(s), in one way or another, to the result of their choice for the rest of their lives. Given careful, loving choices after a pregnancy occurs, along with an attitude of willingness to accept and let the Lord turn hardship into blessing, the lives of the teen(s) and the baby will be forever touched by His loving, forgiving, and fulfilling hand.

May God's peace and joy fill your hearts as He guides

you beyond the current hurts and crises, for He shall help you become a better, stronger person tomorrow for your efforts and faith today.

Our Hand in His

The answers to the following questions may help you sort through some of the issues of having a teenager prepare for and enter into marriage:

1. Have you accepted that your teen is getting married and will be starting a home of her own soon?
2. With this acceptance, have you tried to relax as much as possible and enjoy the pleasurable elements of the occasion?
3. Are you willing to let your teen enjoy the excitement of this time, realizing that the reality of adult life will hit her soon enough?
4. Is your teen aware that you are available if and when she needs to seek your advice?
5. On the other hand, have you vowed to stay out of their way unless asked for help, or until you believe that there is imminent danger that requires your interference (such as physical abuse or child neglect)?
6. If there is a crisis, are you prepared to calmly lead the young couple to professional help, stressing the importance of trying to keep their marriage intact?
7. Have you resolved not to take sides with your teen or her spouse?
8. Have you offered them the promise that you are willing to help as you can, but your main obligation is to *love them alone?*
9. Have you led the teens to Scripture that gives specific instruction on what is expected of husbands and wives (Eph. 4:2; 5:22-33; 1 Pet. 3:1-9; and Phil. 2:2-4)?

10. And are you able to effectively discuss the meaning of the marital partnership according to Scripture (i.e., husband and wife are supposed to serve each other in a true partnership of fulfillment, not tyrannize or abuse each other)?
11. And have you read Philippians 4:6-8? *Do not be anxious about anything, but in everything, by prayer and petition, with thanksgiving, present your requests to God. And the peace of God, which transcends all understanding, will guard your hearts and your minds in Christ Jesus. Finally, brothers, whatever is true, whatever is noble, whatever is right, whatever is pure, whatever is lovely, whatever is admirable—if anything is excellent or praiseworthy—think about such things.*